SOUTHERN
CROSSINGS

GOURMET TRAVELLER

NEW ZEALAND

INSPIRED ESCAPES ✛ CULINARY JOURNEYS

TIAKI PROMISE

Gourmet Traveller and Southern Crossings respect the values of the Tiaki Promise.
Tiaki means to care for people and place. New Zealand is precious, and everyone who lives and travels here
has a responsibility to look after it. The Tiaki Promise is a commitment to care for New Zealand, for now
and for future generations. By following the Tiaki Promise, you are making a commitment to New Zealand.
To act as a guardian, protecting and preserving our home. Nau Mai, Haere Mai Ki Aotearoa,
Welcome to New Zealand.

NEW ZEALAND

INSPIRED ESCAPES ✛ CULINARY JOURNEYS

Under alpine skies

In the vines

CONTENTS

By the coast

On the land

AOTEAROA

The land of the long white cloud is a land like no other. New Zealand's topographically blessed islands make it a treasure trove for both local and international travellers. Te Ika-a-Māui, the Māori name for the North Island, is the magical land of Sir Peter Jackson's *Lord of the Rings* trilogy. Some of the best reds are created at Craggy Range in the Hawke's Bay, and the orchards and farms in the aptly named Bay of Plenty provide a rich bounty. Taonga or treasures abound too, on Te Waipounamu, the South Island, from the natural wonders of the Marlborough Sounds to the spiritual home of sauvignon blanc in Marlborough, and Abel Tasman National Park's native forest and pristine beaches. In this travel cookbook, *Gourmet Traveller* in partnership with Southern Crossings, bring you 21 of New Zealand's most luxurious destinations and offer a taste of the landscape with recipes from each property. While each kitchen reflects the unique produce from their region of Aotearoa, they all embrace local, seasonal and paddock-to-plate dining. So whether you're after a rejuvenating wellness sanctuary at Kaiteriteri in Nelson, a nostalgic beach holiday in an iconic bach on Waiheke Island or an alpine retreat with world-class fly fishing in North Otago's rugged Ahuriri Valley, there's plenty of land and cloud and more to explore. We hope this book will bring you a taste of the unique food and travel treasures of New Zealand and whet your appetite for your next adventure.

Southern Crossings pioneered the concept of bespoke luxury travel to New Zealand in 1986 with its vision to "enrich and inspire by creating extraordinary journeys". The dramatic and varied landscapes of this beautiful part of the world provided the perfect canvas from which to create personally curated itineraries designed for the most discerning of travellers.

More than three decades later, Southern Crossings leads the way in tailoring holidays and unique travel experiences throughout New Zealand, Australia and the South Pacific.

Over the years, luxury travel has evolved and Southern Crossings has embraced this evolution. Today's sophisticated travellers want more than just luxury; they seek authentic, personal experiences that offer a chance to connect with, and positively impact, the people and places they visit.

Southern Crossings' long-standing reputation as New Zealand's trusted travel experts has earned a loyal client following and numerous prestigious industry affiliations. Owners and directors, Sarah Farag and Australian-based Stuart Rigg, are also internationally recognised for their personal travel expertise with a range of awards for their contributions to the industry.

Applying in-depth local knowledge and meticulous dedication to planning, ensures that every Southern Crossings' itinerary is designed to suit the client's individual preferences. Each tailored journey incorporates the combined knowledge, insights and connections of the company's travel design team to curate bespoke luxury travel experiences.

For more than 35 years, the company has been designing memorable journeys for international visitors throughout New Zealand, Australia and

the islands of the South Pacific. The travel design team now also generously share their experience and insights to inspire and delight sophisticated local travellers, who also enjoy the privileges that flow from the strength of Southern Crossings' well-established industry relationships.

Culinary experiences are often at the heart of Southern Crossings' itineraries and the recipes from each of the properties in this book are a testament to the power of food to transport you to another place. Food can inspire curiosity, enliven your journey, and create travel memories to be savoured and treasured. With this in mind, Southern Crossings has created uniquely New Zealand culinary-focused experiences to take you behind the scenes. Whether you choose to dine under star-lit mountain skies or beside the shores of New Zealand's abundant and rugged coastline,

you'll discover a world of flavours to match each unique location.

Through culinary connections that go far beyond the expected, Southern Crossings introduces discerning travellers to award-winning chefs and winemakers as well as the many talented local producers and providores behind some of New Zealand's best-kept culinary secrets. From freshly foraged outdoor picnics and Fiordland feasts through to the finest of fine dining, every part of New Zealand's diverse and scenic landscapes offers a different taste to explore and savour. And that is what Southern Crossings delivers in one-of-a-kind bespoke culinary journeys designed to leave a lasting impression and create treasured travel memories of destinations and their unique flavours and landscapes.
southern-crossings.com

UNDER ALPINE SKIES

Discover the majesty of Aotearoa's rugged mountain landscapes. Explore fly fishing at Ahuriri Valley, mystical Middle Earth territory at Lake Wakatipu and a chalet at World Heritage-listed Mount Aspiring. Go off the grid at a private retreat in the Motueka Valley or immerse yourself in the secluded beauty of a working sheep station at Castle Hill.

The Lindis

Blending seamlessly into the rugged landscape of the Ahuriri Valley
on New Zealand's South Island, this luxury lodge offers the ultimate in
seasonal dining, world-class fly fishing and high country hospitality.

Located on 6000 acres in the pristine Ahuriri Valley, The Lindis is situated on Ben Avon Station in a rugged slice of paradise on New Zealand's South Island. Designed to blend imperceptibly into the valley's dramatic landscape of mountain country, wetlands and beech forest, this luxury lodge with its organic-shaped wood-slatted roof and harmonious design, pays homage to its breathtaking natural surrounds. There's no better place to escape from it all than a place where the quiet of nature becomes amplified and where connecting to the land seems to happen by default.

This celebration of nature is evident throughout The Lindis – from the interior design to the menu – everything draws inspiration from, and respects the land. Designed by Architecture Workshop, the interior reflects the natural environment with spotted gum panelling and bluestone masonry used throughout. Sweeping floor-to-ceiling windows blur the boundaries between the inside and outside. The lodge features two spacious master suites, three luxurious lodge suites, three pods with private outdoor bathtubs, Great Hall dining, a bar, lounge areas and a billiards room, all furnished in natural timber and stone and designed for the ultimate in luxurious comfort. The lodge also offers guests a hot tub, gym and treatment room for rejuvenation.

Dining in the Great Hall is an unforgettable culinary experience with a contemporary and refined take on seasonal New Zealand cuisine. With almost all of its produce sourced locally or harvested from the kitchen's onsite garden, the flavours are an expression of the local terrain. The menu features unique and distinctive natural ingredients such as locally foraged porcini mushrooms and wild Fiordland venison. Paired with the sommelier's careful selection of outstanding local and international wines, the Great Hall offers a series of memorable sensory moments.

Guests can experience the natural beauty of the surrounding Ahuriri Valley with excursions to suit all types of adventurers. For those looking for a little physical activity, try fishing for trout in the Ahuriri River, rated as one of the top five places in the world for fly fishing. Or perhaps a horse ride through the trails with one of the lodge's horses from its stables. For the romantic, try some spectacular stargazing at the lodge as it's blessed with extremely low light pollution in the Ahuriri Valley and some of the clearest night skies.

The Lindis offers its guests genuine high country New Zealand hospitality to match the rugged perfection of the surrounding Ahuriri Valley. All you have to do is immerse yourself in its wonder.

EXPLORE

• Enjoy a high country picnic – from an alpine picnic platter to an Ahuriri Valley barbecue or a mulled wine experience – replete with luxurious white tablecloths, sheepskin rugs and Champagne.

• Go stargazing at The Lindis. With extremely low light pollution in the Ahuriri Valley, the night sky above the lodge is so clear that millions of stars are visible.

Duck and butternut purée with mandarin sauce and cherries

SERVES 4 // PREP TIME 25 MINS // COOK 35 MINS (PLUS PICKLING, RESTING)

"This is the perfect summer dish. With festive spices and aromatic cherries, it really sings of summer," says head chef Dane Archery. "We use Canter Valley duck from North Canterbury and amazing cherries from Cherry Tree Farms, just a stone's throw from the lodge. We also use mint and mizuna from the Lindis garden to add freshness to the sweet and sour tones of this dish." You will need to pickle the cherries two days ahead.

4   duck breasts (240gm each)
    Dill, mint tips and mizuna, to serve

PICKLED CHERRIES
12   cherries, halved, pitted
125   ml apple cider vinegar
1   star anise
5   gm tarragon

BUTTERNUT PURÉE
450   gm butternut pumpkin, peeled and finely chopped
100   gm unsalted butter, chopped
80   ml pouring cream
1   tbsp aged chardonnay vinegar

MANDARIN AND COCONUT SAUCE
500   ml chicken stock
300   ml mandarin juice (see note)
20   gm ginger, thinly sliced
½   cinnamon quill
220   ml coconut cream

1 For pickled cherries, place cherries, vinegar, star anise and tarragon in a glass jar, seal and store in the warmest part of the kitchen. Leave for up to 48 hours and they will last for up to 3 months (see note).

2 On the day of serving, for butternut purée, preheat oven to 200°C. Place butternut pumpkin on an oven tray lined with baking paper, season, then roast until tender (20-25 minutes). Transfer to a saucepan with butter, cream and vinegar, bring to a simmer, stirring until butter is melted. Transfer to a blender and blend until smooth, then season to taste. Keep the oven on for the duck.

3 Meanwhile, for mandarin and coconut sauce, place chicken stock, mandarin juice, ginger and cinnamon quill in a saucepan over medium heat and cook until reduced by three-quarters and thick enough to coat the back of a spoon (25 minutes). Add coconut cream and simmer until thick enough to coat the back of a spoon (2-3 minutes). Strain, then season to taste with pepper (we use pink peppercorns, but black will do just fine).

4 For duck, score the duck breast skin lightly with a sharp knife then season both sides generously with salt. Place duck breasts, skin-side down, in a cold ovenproof frying pan. Place pan over medium heat without any oil and cook until the skin is crisp underneath (4 minutes). Turn over, then transfer the pan to the oven and roast until medium-rare (6 minutes). Remove and rest, covered, on a cool oven tray for 3 minutes. Carve each duck breast into three or four slices.

5 To serve, divide butternut purée among plates, then top with duck. Spoon around mandarin and coconut sauce. Garnish with pickled cherries then finish each plate with dill, mint tips and mizuna.

NOTE For mandarin juice, you will need 8 mandarins. The pickled cherries' flavour improves with keeping. Any leftovers can be paired with a cheese board or to accompany other roast poultry.

PREPARE AHEAD Butternut purée and mandarin and coconut sauce can be made a day ahead.

WINE MATCH 2016 Ostler Caroline's Pinot Noir, Waitaki Valley.

Octopus carpaccio with Paroa Bay raisins, hazelnuts and olive oil

SERVES 4 // PREP TIME 30 MINS // COOK 25 MINS (PLUS OVERNIGHT MACERATING, INFUSING, CHILLING)

"We are very lucky to source our octopus from Tim Barnett from Ocean Speared, a spear-fishing company that produces zero bycatch, does zero trawling and targets lesser-known species," says Archery. "The hazelnuts and olive oil that we use in this dish come from Jocelyn Robinson and Sandy Black, owner-operators of Dunford Grove in Cromwell. It is very important to us to buy food from people, not brands, and I urge you to do the same to improve the quality of your food." You will need to macerate the raisins a day ahead.

2 tbsp extra-virgin olive oil
Juice of 1 lemon
1 long red chilli, cut into julienne
Zest of 1 orange
2 tbsp dry-roasted skinless hazelnuts, chopped
1 spring onion, green part only, cut into julienne

MACERATED RAISINS
75 gm Paroa Bay (or golden) raisins
80 ml rosé
1½ tsp thyme leaves
2 nori sheets

OCTOPUS
2 tsp black peppercorns
1 lemon, halved, thinly sliced
1 orange, halved, thinly sliced
8 saffron threads
3 tsp caster sugar
20 gm fine salt
1 kg large octopus tentacles

NORI SALT
1 nori sheet
50 gm sea salt flakes

1 For macerated raisins, place ingredients in a glass jar, seal and leave to macerate overnight (see note).

2 For octopus, place ingredients, except octopus, and 2 litres of water in a large, heavy-based saucepan. Bring to the boil, reduce heat to medium and simmer to develop flavours (15 minutes). Add octopus tentacles, return to the boil, then reduce heat to low and cook for 8 minutes. Turn off the heat and leave the octopus to cool in the liquid (20 minutes). Strain, then refrigerate octopus for at least 1 hour. Discard peppercorns and citrus slices.

3 For nori salt, hold nori sheet with tongs and toast over a gas flame until it smells distinctly roasted (5-10 seconds). Cool, then place in a blender with salt and blend to a fine powder. Alternatively, grind using a mortar and pestle. Transfer to a jar then store in the freezer until required (see note).

4 To serve, slice tentacles as thinly as possible, divide and arrange among plates with the macerated raisins. Drizzle with extra-virgin olive oil and lemon juice. Season with nori salt and freshly ground pepper to taste, then sprinkle with chilli, orange zest, hazelnuts and spring onion.

NOTE Leftover macerated raisins will keep for up to 6 months refrigerated and are useful for anywhere a touch of sweetness is needed. You can halve the nori salt recipe, if preferred. The nori salt adds a kick of umami to almost any dish and will elevate a piece of steak or poached egg.

PREPARE AHEAD Octopus can be prepared up to a day ahead.

WINE MATCH 2019 Paroa Bay Syrah, Northland.

Blanket Bay

This luxury alpine lodge on picturesque Lake Wakatipu is the ideal place to discover the region's ocean-to-alps dining, wilderness adventures and its magical Middle Earth landscape.

Set on the magnificent, glacier-carved Lake Wakatipu 40 minutes' drive from Queenstown in the South Island, Blanket Bay is the perfect place to experience some of New Zealand's most exhilarating wilderness adventures. This magical landscape has also garnered fame as the location of Middle Earth immortalised in Sir Peter Jackson's *Lord of the Rings* film trilogy.

Blanket Bay is located within Wyuna Station, which at 10,000 acres is one of New Zealand's larger high country stations. It was named after the blanket shed and shelters constructed by Māori shearers to protect themselves and their sheep more than a century ago, when mobs of sheep were shorn on the shores of Lake Wakatipu in a bay just south of Glenorchy.

Besides alpine mountains and lakes on its doorstep, swimming pools, hot tubs, spa therapy suites, sprawling grounds, and kilometres of trails, Blanket Bay's cuisine offers a standout experience that sets this lodge apart. The Blanket Bay kitchen promotes the region's finest produce including the meat from its own sheep, beef and bounty from the farm on Wyuna Station. Although surrounded by the Southern Alps, the lodge lies less than 50 kilometres from Fiordland's coast so that the freshest catch appears on its daily changing dégustation dinner menu, making it a true ocean-to-alps culinary offering. Complemented by an impressive list of local and international wines, meals are served either in the formal dining room, the intimate wine cave or on the terrace by the glow of a huge outdoor fireplace.

Built in 1999 by owners Tom and Pauline Tusher, the lodge features reclaimed hardwood wharf and bridge beams, locally quarried stone and Welsh slate. It is unrivalled for access to both Mount Aspiring and Fiordland World Heritage sites. At the heart of the lodge lies the Great Room and Den where guests gather for a pre-dinner aperitif by the fireplace and take in the sweeping lake views.

Accommodation includes three sumptuous Lodge suites with separate bedroom and sitting areas, stone fireplaces, steam showers and separate tubs. Standalone Chalets, designed to reflect New Zealand's colonial architecture, complement the main lodge through the use of schist stone and timber beams. The Villa offers the ultimate private sanctuary with four king suites.

Explore the area with guided fly fishing, heli-flights to World Heritage site Milford Sound, jet boating on the Dart River or cycling and hiking in Mount Aspiring National Park. Blanket Bay also offers horse riding on the adjoining Wyuna High Country Station, and in winter the lodge is the perfect base for heli-skiing with a qualified guide.

EXPLORE

• Request a tour of the Tasting Room before selecting a bottle of wine for dinner. With 250 bottles in its collection, the Cellar List is reserved for a premium one-off experience.

• Explore the magnificent World Heritage area of Fiordland, less than 50 kilometres away, on a helicopter tour from Blanket Bay's private pad on its front lawn.

Fallow deer, Bourbon-glazed pineapple, cavolo nero, spiced jus and fennel butter

SERVES 4 // PREP TIME 50 MINS // COOK 30 MINS (PLUS RESTING)

"We love showcasing the wild Central Otago fallow deer on our menus regularly," says head chef Daniel Reynolds. "As Blanket Bay is at the heart of the rugged Humboldt Mountains, we find it fitting to use this great product. We match it with barbecued pineapple as it adds a freshness and smokiness that complements the wild game flavour."

Grapeseed oil, for deep-frying and sautéing
12 small cavolo nero leaves
Venison jus (see note), to serve

FENNEL BUTTER
½ tsp fennel seeds
125 gm unsalted butter, softened
2 tsp finely chopped fennel fronds

BOURBON-GLAZED PINEAPPLE
200 ml Bourbon
50 gm caster sugar
50 ml pineapple juice
1 star anise
1 cinnamon quill
3 cloves
750 gm pineapple (about ¾ small pineapple), peeled

FALLOW DEER
8 large cavolo nero leaves, stems removed
16 prosciutto slices
4 wild deer (venison) short-loin portions (120gm each; see note)

1 For fennel butter, place fennel seeds in a frying pan and dry-roast over medium heat (1-2 minutes) or until toasted. Cool, then blend in a spice grinder or with a mortar and pestle to a powder. Place ground fennel, butter and fennel fronds in a food processor and process until smooth. Transfer to a container and store at room temperature until required.

2 For crisp cavolo nero leaves, heat oil in a deep saucepan to 180°C. In batches, carefully fry leaves until crisp (1 minute). Drain on paper towel and season.

3 For Bourbon-glazed pineapple, place Bourbon in a small saucepan over medium heat then carefully flambé. Shake the pan occasionally until flames subside. Add remaining ingredients, except pineapple, and simmer until reduced to a syrup consistency (6 minutes). Set aside to cool.

4 Cut pineapple into four 1cm-thick rounds. Using a pastry cutter, cut out the core and discard. Glaze pineapple with Bourbon syrup. Heat a char-grill pan (or frying pan) over medium heat. Cook pineapple until golden (4 minutes each side). Set aside.

5 For fallow deer, blanch cavolo nero leaves in boiling water for 10 seconds, drain and refresh in iced water. Place four slices of prosciutto, side by side, on a chopping board slightly overlapping and two cavolo nero leaves on top. Top with a short-loin piece and roll up so the prosciutto is on the outside. Repeat with remaining prosciutto, cavolo nero and venison. Preheat oven to 180°C. Heat a little grapeseed oil in a large frying pan over medium-high heat, add venison and cook, turning, until browned and prosciutto is crisp (5-6 minutes). Transfer to an oven tray and roast for 5 minutes for medium-rare. Remove from the oven and rest for 5 minutes. Cut each portion into three pieces.

6 To serve, divide pineapple among plates, add sliced venison, garnish with fried cavolo nero and a quenelle of fennel butter. Finish with jus, if using, or resting juices.

NOTE If venison jus is unavailable, use a lightly flavoured jus or pan juices from resting the venison. Wild deer short loin from Central Otago is a very tender cut. If it's unavailable, substitute lamb.

PREPARE AHEAD Fennel butter and Bourbon glaze can be made a day ahead. Bring butter to room temperature before using.

WINE MATCH 2019 Maude Wines Poison Creek Single Vineyard Pinot Noir, Wānaka.

Spring rhubarb consommé, rhubarb compote and crumble

SERVES 6 // PREP TIME 30 MINS // COOK 35 MINS (PLUS SETTING, CHILLING)

"This is our take on a traditional rhubarb crumble," says Reynolds. **"Served cold, it adds a freshness to this classic dish as well as a nice twist for our guests. Spring is when rhubarb comes into season in New Zealand, and this is the perfect way to use this vibrant and colourful fruit."**

Vanilla ice-cream, to serve
Edible flowers, to garnish

RHUBARB CONSOMMÉ
250 gm rhubarb stalks, cut into
    2cm pieces
250 ml water

RHUBARB COMPOTE
250 gm rhubarb stalks, cut into
    2cm pieces
  2 tbsp water
 70 gm caster sugar
1½ gold-strength gelatine leaves
 ¼ tsp agar agar powder (see note)
  1 tsp caster sugar, extra

CRUMBLE DISCS
 50 gm unsalted butter,
    at room temperature
 40 gm caster sugar
 16 gm demerara sugar
 60 gm strong flour

1 For rhubarb consommé, place rhubarb and water in a large saucepan and cook over medium heat until tender (5 minutes). Strain through a fine sieve into a bowl, leaving mixture to drip through. Do not push the rhubarb or it will cloud the rhubarb consommé. Discard solids and stand until cooled.

2 For rhubarb compote, preheat oven to 190°C. Combine rhubarb, water and sugar in an ovenproof glass or ceramic dish. Cover with foil and roast until tender (12-15 minutes). Cool then strain liquid into a saucepan. Reserve rhubarb.

3 Meanwhile, soak gelatine leaves in a bowl of cold water until softened (3 minutes). Squeeze out excess water, then add bloomed gelatine and combined agar agar and extra sugar to the saucepan with rhubarb liquid from step 2. Place the pan over medium heat and simmer, stirring until gelatine and sugar dissolve (2 minutes). Remove the pan from heat, then fold in cooked reserved rhubarb until it starts to collapse. Line a tray with baking paper. Grease six 7cm metal ring moulds, then line bases with plastic wrap and secure with a rubber band. Place moulds on the lined tray. Divide rhubarb compote among moulds and refrigerate until firm (1 hour) or until ready to serve.

4 For crumble discs, preheat oven to 190°C. Place ingredients in a food processor and process until mixture forms very small even crumbs. Place crumb mixture on an oven tray lined with baking paper and freeze until firm (30 minutes). Process frozen clusters in a food processor to a coarse powder and return to the fridge until required. Grease six 7cm metal ring moulds and place on an oven tray lined with baking paper. Place 1 tbsp mixture into each mould. Bake until lightly golden (6-8 minutes). Carefully lift the ring moulds from the crumble discs.

5 To serve, unmould a rhubarb compote into each bowl. Top with a crumble disc, then place a quenelle of vanilla ice-cream on top. Garnish with an edible flower, then pour in rhubarb consommé.

NOTE Agar agar, a gelling agent derived from seaweed, is available from Asian grocers.

PREPARE AHEAD Recipe can be made a day ahead. Leftover crumble can be frozen for another use. Leftover compote will keep refrigerated for up to 1 week.

WINE MATCH 2014 Seresin Moana Sparkling Rosé, Marlborough.

Minaret Station

A secluded luxury alpine lodge in the Southern Alps offers
off-the-beaten-track adventures, paddock-to-plate dining and a chance
to disconnect from the outside world in a private chalet.

Accessible only by helicopter, Minaret Station Alpine Lodge is one of the most secluded luxury lodges in the world, with just four private chalets. Located in a glacial valley, Minaret Station is set among the untouched beauty of the Southern Alps next to World Heritage-listed Mount Aspiring National Park. Bordered by national parks, mountains and Lake Wānaka, there are no roads to the lodge which makes it the perfect alpine hideaway.

Each chalet is decorated in high-country style and features its own king-size bed, ensuite and private deck with a hot tub, where guests can relax and unwind beneath the stars. Guests can choose to dine with others in the Mountain Kitchen's dining room, the library with the open fireplace, alfresco on the deck, or in the privacy of their own chalet.

The chefs at Minaret Station follow a paddock-to-plate ethos, using only the freshest local ingredients from Central Otago's basin. The menu's venison, Lumina lamb and Angus beef are all sourced from Minaret Station's own 50,000-acre working farm. Seafood is fresh from Stewart Island, the West Coast and Fiordland. The Central Otago region provides an optimal environment for distinctive seasonal produce. The region's cool winters and hot dry summers provide prime growing conditions, allowing local suppliers to produce an abundance of delicious stone fruit, berries, mānuka honey and vegetables. The menu remains true to the region's flavours with a simple yet refined style. Highlights include Fiordland crayfish omelette, 12-hour slow-braised Lumina lamb shoulder, Minaret Station venison tartare with mānuka smoked macadamia nuts. An extensive list of fine New Zealand wines from boutique winemakers complements the menu. In summer, try the Bee's Knees cocktail – a zesty combination of The Source Gin, lemon juice and locally sourced honey.

All water used in the Alpine Lodge comes from annual rainfall and snowmelt. The drinking water is drawn from the snow- and rain-fed waterfall behind the Alpine Lodge and is 100 per cent pure New Zealand water.

A private guide is included with every stay providing guests the opportunity to explore the many hiking trails at the doorstep of the lodge. Guided experiences take guests beyond the beaten path to explore the beauty of Fiordland, Milford Sound, Dusky Sound, Aoraki Mt Cook and many national parks. Minaret Station also offers authentic experiences throughout New Zealand's South Island including an extensive range of helicopter touring, hiking, backcountry fly fishing, guided hunting and heli-skiing.

EXPLORE

• Look out for the wild deer that roam through the valley at dusk and dawn from the comfort of your chalet's private deck.

• Minaret Station Alpine Lodge is powered by hydro-electricity which is fed by the natural waterfall above the lodge.

Slow-cooked lamb shoulder, cucumber salsa, pistachio dukkah, labne and salad

SERVES 4-6 // PREP TIME 30 MINS // COOK 5 HRS 45 MINS (PLUS OVERNIGHT DRAINING, RESTING)

"This recipe uses Greek and Middle Eastern-style flavours," says executive chef Alastair Wilson. "Spiced labne and a crisp cucumber salsa with salad greens are perfect to balance the richness of the lamb." You will need to make the labne a day ahead.

1 oyster-cut lamb shoulder (1.4-1.6kg; see note)
2 tsp finely chopped thyme
1 tbsp cumin seeds, toasted
1 tbsp fennel seeds, toasted
2 garlic gloves, crushed
1 long red chilli, seeds removed, sliced
2 large golden shallots, chopped
1 litre unsalted chicken stock

LABNE
300 gm Greek-style yoghurt
2 garlic cloves, finely chopped
Grated rind and juice of 1 lemon
½ tsp ground cumin
½ tsp ground coriander
½ tsp smoked paprika
1 tbsp slivered pistachios
2 tsp sesame seeds, toasted
1 tbsp extra-virgin olive oil, to serve

CUCUMBER SALSA
2 Lebanese cucumbers, seeds removed, diced
55 gm currants, soaked in warm water for 30 minutes, drained
1 small red onion, thinly sliced
50 gm pine nuts, toasted
1 long red chilli, seeds removed, diced
⅓ cup finely chopped mint
⅓ cup finely chopped coriander
Finely grated rind and juice of 1 lime

SALAD GREENS
130 gm mixed salad greens (see note)
1½ tbsp lemon juice
60 ml extra-virgin olive oil

1 For labne, place yoghurt in a sieve lined with muslin set over a bowl. Cover and refrigerate overnight until thick (discard liquid). Add garlic, lemon rind and juice, season to taste and combine well. In a separate bowl, combine dry-roasted spices (see note), pistachios and sesame seeds. Set aside until required.

2 For lamb shoulder, preheat oven to 180°C. Season lamb with salt and freshly ground black pepper and sprinkle with thyme. Heat a large frying pan over medium heat and add lamb, skin-side down. Cook until browned on all sides (8-10 minutes).

3 Transfer lamb, skin-side up, to a roasting pan. Coarsely crush cumin and fennel seeds with a mortar and pestle. Combine seeds with garlic then press onto lamb. Scatter with chilli and shallots then pour the chicken stock around the lamb. Cover with foil and cook for 45 minutes. Reduce temperature to 140°C and cook lamb until very tender and meat is almost falling off the bone (4-4½ hours). Uncover lamb, increase temperature to 190°C and cook until skin is crisp (20 minutes).

4 For cucumber salsa, combine ingredients in a bowl and season to taste.

5 For salad greens, place salad in a bowl, drizzle with lemon juice and olive oil. Season to taste and toss to combine.

6 To serve, place labne in a bowl, top with pistachio dukkah and drizzle with extra-virgin olive oil. Transfer lamb with cooking juices to a serving dish and serve with labne, cucumber salsa and salad greens.

NOTE An oyster-cut of lamb is the blade bone but with the fore shank removed. For the salad greens, we used a mix of baby kale leaves and rocket leaves. To achieve the best flavour for the labne, dry-roast cumin and coriander seeds, then grind with a mortar and pestle.

WINE MATCH 2019 Ata Rangi Célèbre Merlot, Syrah, Malbec and Cabernet Franc, Martinborough.

Fiordland crayfish tail, parsnip purée, lemon brown butter, daikon and smoked macadamias

SERVES 4 // PREP TIME 30 MINS // COOK 45 MINS (PLUS COOLING)

"The hero of this dish is the crayfish. It's not overcooked, we use low temperatures. This keeps the flesh tender," says Wilson.

4 crayfish (100gm each), peeled, veins removed, at room temperature
1 small green apple, shaved
6 smoked macadamias (see note), shaved
Dill sprigs and pea tendrils, to serve

PICKLED DAIKON SALAD
150 gm daikon (about ¼ small daikon), sliced on a mandolin into discs
100 ml chardonnay vinegar
30 gm caster sugar
100 ml water
50 ml cooking sake
50 ml mirin

PARSNIP PURÉE
4 parsnips (150gm each)
50 gm butter
1 golden shallot, finely sliced
2 garlic cloves, finely sliced
1 litre vegetable stock
150 ml pouring cream

BROWN BUTTER
150 gm butter, chopped
Juice of 1 lemon

1 For pickled daikon salad, place daikon in a small heatproof bowl and lightly season with salt. Place vinegar, sugar, water, sake and mirin in a small saucepan and bring to the boil, stirring occasionally until sugar dissolves. Remove from heat, pour over daikon and set aside to cool and pickle.

2 Meanwhile, for parsnip purée, peel parsnips, then cut out and discard the woody core. Cut parsnip into 2cm dice. Melt butter in a saucepan over low heat, add shallot and garlic and cook, stirring until softened (3 minutes). Stir in parsnip and season to taste. Add vegetable stock, bring to a simmer, then reduce heat to low. Cook until parsnip has no resistance when tested with a paring knife (25-30 minutes). Drain well, reserving stock. Return parsnip to the same pan, add 75ml cream and cook over medium heat until cream is reduced by half (1-2 minutes). Transfer parsnip mixture to a blender and blend on low speed, gradually increasing the speed. With the motor running, add the remaining cream. Blend until purée is smooth and thin with a little reserved stock if necessary. Season to taste, then return to the pan and keep warm.

3 Meanwhile, for brown butter, heat butter in a small frying pan over high heat and cook until foaming and nut brown (2-3 minutes). Add crayfish tails and cook, turning, until just tender (4 minutes), then add the lemon juice.

4 To serve, drain daikon from pickling liquid and combine in a bowl with apple. Place a large spoonful of parsnip purée on each plate and top with a crayfish tail. Season crayfish and spoon over brown butter sauce. Place daikon salad alongside the crayfish and garnish with shaved macadamias, dill and pea tendrils.

NOTE Smoked macadamias are available online; alternatively, use dry-roasted macadamias.

PREPARE AHEAD Pickled daikon salad can be made a day ahead.

WINE MATCH 2020 Fromm Clayvin Vineyard Chardonnay, Marlborough.

Falcon Brae Villa

Connect with nature at this off-the-grid private sanctuary on the South Island with its wilderness and high country walking trails, paddock-to-plate dining and uninterrupted mountain and river views.

Perched on a hilltop high above Stonefly Lodge near Nelson and Abel Tasman National Park on the South Island, Falcon Brae Villa is the ultimate off-the-grid retreat for those seeking total privacy. Located on 350 acres of property surrounded on two sides by rivers, including a private forest and spectacular native bush walks, the villa has captivating 360-degree views of the surrounding mountains and the majestic Motueka River.

The villa with its three suites and bunkbed room offers accommodation for up to 10 guests making it ideal for a multigenerational family or those looking for a decadently spacious retreat. The entire villa can be booked for exclusive use with a private chef and house staff. Larger groups can book both the villa and Stonefly Lodge for a total capacity of 14 adults and four children. Each of the villa's suites and deck offers uninterrupted views of Kahurangi National Park and the Motueka River.

The architecturally designed residence features a large central lounge area with a soaring five-metre ceiling, sunken bar, grand piano, media theatre, commercial kitchen, three dining areas and a curated collection of New Zealand art.

Within an hour's drive guests can explore Abel Tasman National Park to the north and Nelson Lakes National Park to the south with walking trails in coastal, wilderness and high country environments. There is also plenty to do onsite with archery, a golf chipping range and 18 kilometres of walking trails through native forest, mature pine forest, grassland and river trails to explore. Guests can enjoy the facilities in the Games Den with its gym, pool table, table tennis, darts and games table. The large deck is perfect for entertainment with its pool, outdoor heated spa and barbecue area for alfresco dining.

Dining at the villa is centred around the fresh produce grown in the kitchen garden and orchards set up by Stonefly Lodge owners John and Kate Kerr. The chef's menu is inspired by both the villa's garden and local producers on Neudorf Road, halfway between Nelson and Motueka. Regional produce such as strawberries, wild mushrooms, truffles, olives, black garlic, smallgoods and charcuterie, cheese and award-winning wines often appear on the menu. The onsite garden and orchards yield a range of produce including figs, quinces, apples, plums, peaches, olives, feijoas, chestnuts, walnuts, tomatoes, chillies, herbs and raspberries. There are also beehives and grapevines. The kitchen's commitment to its paddock-to-plate philosophy is so strong that the villa's orchards and gardens will be extended to yield 100 per cent of the kitchen's produce with excess preserved for off-season use.

EXPLORE

• Overlooking Motueka River, Falcon Brae offers some of the best wild brown New Zealand trout fly fishing. Or try heli-fishing in the nearby Kahurangi National Park in its remote high country wilderness streams.

• The villa's onsite trails range from gentle riverbank walks to bush or forest hikes. Located between three major national parks, Falcon Brae is also within an hour's drive to acclaimed walking trails.

Wild venison, grilled red cabbage, kūmara and prune purée

SERVES 6 // PREP TIME 15 MINS // COOK 1 HR 45 MINS (PLUS PICKLING, RESTING)

"Wild venison is synonymous with New Zealand and our hunting and fishing ethos," says executive chef Michael McMeeken. **"We source it from Premium Game in Marlborough. I treat it simply and season it with a pine needle powder to tie it to its environment."**

GRILLED RED CABBAGE

½ **small red cabbage (600gm)**
Extra-virgin olive oil
150 **ml port**
200 **ml red wine**

PICKLED RED CABBAGE

50 **gm red cabbage trimmings (from recipe above)**
100 **ml water**
100 **ml red wine vinegar**
2 **tsp fine salt**
1 **tsp caster sugar**
1 **small garlic clove, crushed**
3 **black peppercorns**

PRUNE PURÉE

2 **tbsp brandy**
100 **gm prunes**
180 **ml water**
1 **small cinnamon quill**
1 **bay leaf**

ROASTED KŪMARA

2 **small purple or orange kūmara, peeled (400gm)**
1 **tbsp extra-virgin olive oil**
½ **tsp ground star anise**

GREEN BEANS

18 **baby green beans (120gm), halved lengthways**
Extra-virgin olive oil, to cook

VENISON

1 **kg wild venison loin, at room temperature**
2 **tbsp extra-virgin olive oil**
80 **gm butter**
3 **garlic cloves, peeled, bruised**
250 **ml venison jus (see note)**

1 For grilled red cabbage, preheat a char-grill plate or barbecue to medium. Preheat oven to 180°C. Cut cabbage into six equal wedges, keeping the core intact. Remove any loose outer leaves and reserve 50gm for pickling. Lightly oil and season the cabbage. Place on the grill and cook until dark char marks appear, rotate 90 degrees and repeat until both sides have perpendicular grill marks (4-5 minutes each side). Place the grilled cabbage on an oven tray just large enough to fit snuggly without excess space. Drizzle with port and wine, cover with baking paper then cover tray tightly with foil. Bake until tender and the wine has reduced (1 hour).

2 Meanwhile, for pickled red cabbage, trim 50gm reserved cabbage leaves into small organic shapes. Place the water, vinegar, salt, sugar, garlic and peppercorns in a small saucepan over medium heat. Bring to the boil, stirring to dissolve sugar. Add cabbage trimmings, remove from the heat and set aside (1½ hours or until required).

3 For prune purée, place brandy in a heavy-based saucepan over medium-high heat and simmer until reduced by a quarter (1 minute). Add prunes, water, cinnamon and bay leaf. Reduce heat to low and cook until prunes are soft (30 minutes). Discard bay leaf and cinnamon. Place prune mixture in a blender and blend until smooth, then pass through a fine sieve into a bowl. Season to taste, then transfer to a squeeze bottle until required.

4 For roasted kūmara, preheat oven to 180°C. Cut kūmara into 1cm-thick slices, then cut out discs with a 4cm pastry cutter. Place discs in a bowl with olive oil and star anise. Season to taste and toss to combine. Place in a single layer on an oven tray then roast until soft (20 minutes). Keep warm.

5 For green beans, bring a large saucepan of salted water to the boil. Add the beans to the pan and cook until just tender (1 minute), drain and refresh in a bowl of iced water. Drain and set aside until required.

6 For venison, cut venison into three pieces and season to taste just before cooking. Heat a cast-iron skillet or large heavy-based frying pan over medium-high heat. Add oil to the pan, then sear venison until browned all over (10 minutes). Add butter and garlic. Baste with the foaming butter, turning on all sides, and cook until the desired doneness is achieved (approximately 3-5 minutes for rare venison). Rest, covered, for 5 minutes in a warm place.

7 To serve, place the blanched beans in a hot dry frying pan or on a char-grill plate with olive oil and toss to blacken. Season to taste. Place a grilled cabbage wedge and three kūmara discs on each plate. Dot prune purée on kūmara discs, then add green beans. Place six pieces of pickled red cabbage on the vegetables. Slice the venison and season. Place venison on each plate and finish with jus.

NOTE If venison jus is unavailable, use a lightly flavoured beef jus or the pan juices from resting the venison.

PREPARE AHEAD Pickled red cabbage can be made a day ahead.

WINE MATCH 2020 Rippon Gamay, Wānaka.

Summer berry trifle, berry gelée, crème fraîche ice-cream

SERVES 8 // PREP TIME 2½ HRS // COOK 40 MINS (PLUS CHILLING, COOLING, SETTING)

"This elevated berry trifle is inspired by my childhood," says McMeeken. "It was my go-to birthday dessert and a feature on the Christmas day table. My mum's recipe was a classic version of trifle, and it's still one of my favourite desserts."

100 ml brandy, sherry, or rum
Berries (see note), to serve

CRÈME FRAÎCHE ICE-CREAM
4 egg yolks
1 whole egg
60 gm caster sugar
40 ml dessert wine
200 gm crème fraîche

BERRY COULIS
1 kg berries (see note)
Zest and juice of 1 lemon
1 vanilla bean, split, seeds scraped
100 gm icing sugar, sieved

VANILLA CAKE
165 gm baker's flour
1½ tsp baking powder
115 gm softened butter
275 gm caster sugar
3 eggs
½ tsp vanilla paste
150 ml buttermilk

BERRY GELÉE
4½ titanium-strength gelatine leaves
450 ml berry liquid (from berry coulis)
1 tbsp lemon juice

SUMMER BERRY MOUSSE
200 gm berry coulis
3 titanium-strength gelatine leaves
2 tsp lemon juice
1 egg white
30 gm caster sugar
160 ml pouring cream

1 For crème fraîche ice-cream, whisk egg yolks, egg, sugar and wine in a heatproof bowl until sugar dissolves. Place the bowl over a saucepan of gently simmering water (bowl should fit snugly over pan) and whisk continuously until mixture is tripled in volume and holds a ribbon (8-10 minutes). Place the bowl over a bowl of iced water and whisk until cool. Whisk in crème fraîche until incorporated then churn in an ice-cream machine until frozen. Transfer to a container and freeze until required. Makes 500ml.

2 For berry coulis, place ingredients in a heavy-based saucepan over medium-high heat. Cook, covered, stirring frequently until sugar dissolves, then simmer, uncovered, until berries break down (4-5 minutes). Strain berries through a sieve, reserving the berry liquid for gelée (you will need 450ml liquid). Blend strained berries in a blender until smooth, then press through a fine sieve and discard seeds. Makes about 400gm coulis. Place 100gm coulis in a squeeze bottle; reserve 200gm coulis for the summer berry mousse and 100gm to brush over the vanilla cake.

3 For vanilla cake, preheat oven to 180°C, grease and line a 25cm x 37cm oven tray with baking paper. Sift flour, baking powder and a pinch of salt into a bowl. Beat butter and sugar in an electric mixer until light and fluffy. Add eggs one at a time, beating well between each addition. Add vanilla paste and beat until combined. Fold in dry ingredients alternately with buttermilk. Spread into prepared tray, smooth top, then bake until cake is golden and an inserted skewer withdraws clean (15-20 minutes). Cool in the tin for 10 minutes, then invert onto a wire rack lined with baking paper. Cool completely.

4 For berry gelée, soak gelatine leaves in a bowl of cold water until softened (3 minutes). Meanwhile, place 450ml reserved berry liquid in a small saucepan over medium heat and bring to a simmer. Squeeze out excess water from gelatine, add to the pan and stir until gelatine dissolves. Remove from heat and stir in lemon juice. Strain into a bowl and set aside at room temperature until required.

5 For summer berry mousse, place 200gm berry coulis in a saucepan and heat until warmed. Meanwhile, soak gelatine leaves in a bowl of cold water until softened (3 minutes). Squeeze out excess water, add to the pan and stir until gelatine dissolves. Remove from heat, stir in lemon juice then strain through a sieve into a large bowl and cool. Whisk egg white to soft peaks with a balloon whisk. Gradually add sugar and whisk to stiff peaks, then fold meringue into coulis in two batches. Place cream in a clean bowl and whisk to soft peaks with an electric mixer, then fold into berry mixture until just combined.

6 To assemble trifle, line a 20cm square cake tin with baking paper, extending paper above tin rim. Trim vanilla sponge to fit tin and place to cover tin base. Brush sponge with brandy, then 100gm reserved berry coulis. Top with mousse and level with an offset spatula. Refrigerate until set (2 hours). Top mousse with a 2mm-thick layer of berry gelée. Refrigerate until set (1 hour).

7 To serve, using the baking paper, lift trifle from tin onto a chopping board and cut into eight equal rectangles. Divide trifle among plates, garnish with berries and dots of coulis. Finish with a quenelle of crème fraîche ice-cream.

NOTE Summer berries that can be used are blackberries, cherries, raspberries and strawberries.

PREPARE AHEAD Recipe can be made a day ahead.

WINE MATCH 2018 Villa Maria Reserve Noble Riesling Botrytis Selection, Marlborough.

Flockhill Homestead

Architecturally designed to resemble a minimalist farm shed,
this homestead on a working sheep station harmonises with nature
as an exquisite and secluded hideaway in the Southern Alps.

Named after the flock of sheep that graze on the station, Flockhill Homestead offers guests a welcome respite from the rugged landscape of the working sheep station on which it stands. Designed by Warren and Mahoney Architects, the homestead reflects the raw beauty of the surrounding limestone cliffs with a harmonious mix of limestone and timber used throughout. Built to resemble a farm shed, its floor-to-ceiling windows capture the dramatic landscape with views of Lake Pearson, Sugar Loaf, Purple Hill and beyond. The homestead is a simple pitched roof pavilion with large central living areas and separate guest quarters on either side. With this free-flowing design, there is a seamless connection between the internal and external spaces. The homestead is a sanctuary that capitalises on the natural beauty of its surroundings with no compromise on luxury.

Accommodation includes four elegant suites with luxurious spaces to sleep, write, sit and literally soak up the view while bathing. Each room features a gas fireplace, walk-in wardrobes and a place to sit and relax.

The lounge and dining room with its wood-burning fireplace is sumptuous yet expansive and ideal for entertaining. Guests can choose from a selection of local and international wines clearly visible in the temperature-controlled custom wine cellar. A sitting room-cum-games room with hidden bar is perfect for an aperitif or an after-dinner drink. The den provides a modern playlist along with a popular retro vinyl collection.

Dining at the homestead is an ever-changing culinary experience as the chef discusses the daily offering in the farm-style kitchen. Menus are based on local, seasonal produce either from the farm or local artisan producers.

The homestead's stratified concrete and beech timber finish with limestone floors softened by silk and merino rugs create a sense of understated pared-back luxury. The expansive glass doors that open onto the terrace not only highlight the view but entice you to enjoy the outdoor spa, pool and fire pit. A walled barbecue area to escape the elements provides the ideal space for the chef to create an alfresco feast.

A tour of the Merino Romneys with the station manager and his dog is a highlight, while hiking or mountain biking on the property is a good way to take in the vast landscape. Thrill-seekers can try adrenaline-charged caving in nearby Craigieburn Valley's subterranean Cave Stream. A visit to Kura Tāwhiti or Castle Hill is a must for those seeking a more meaningful connection to the place once named by the Dalai Lama as the "spiritual centre of the universe".

EXPLORE

• Explore the 36,000-acre working sheep station on horseback through open grassland, beech forest, streams, mānuka scrub, and tussock valleys.

• Visit Lake Pearson or Ōpōrea, a high-country lake in the Waimakariri basin on the edge of Flockhill Station. It is a wildlife refuge for the southern crested grebe. Māori call these protected birds kāmana and regard them as taonga or treasure.

Flounder with caper butter

SERVES 4 // PREP TIME 30 MINS // COOK 50 MINS (PLUS SOAKING, INFUSING)

"Pātiki is the New Zealand native sand flounder," says chef Taylor Cullen. "This delicate flaky flat fish deserves to be treated simply. I cook it in a cast-iron pan, seasoned with local sea salt in a fire with mānuka wood. To finish the dish, I use sea kelp, katsuobushi, capers and herbs picked from our garden which results in a true umami taste – the essence of deliciousness."

160 ml extra-virgin olive oil
4 large flounder (about 500gm each), cleaned
  Steamed green beans, lemon cheeks and nasturtium leaves, to serve

BONITO ICHIBAN DASHI
10 gm kombu
2 litres water
15 gm katsuobushi (see note)

CAPER BUTTER
250 gm unsalted butter, chopped
50 gm soft mixed herbs (see note), coarsely chopped
⅛ tsp xanthan gum
80 gm baby capers

1 For bonito ichiban dashi, combine kombu and water in a bowl, and soak for 4 hours or overnight. Place the mixture in a saucepan and place over medium heat until it reaches 65°C. Hold it at this temperature for 10 minutes, ensuring it doesn't come to the boil (boiling kombu can lead to undesirable flavours and brings out a gelatinous character). When done, you should be able to pierce the kombu. Remove the kombu with a slotted spoon. Reheat 200ml kombu dashi to 80°C, reserving the remaining kombu dashi for another recipe. Add katsuobushi to the pan, then remove from the heat and infuse (10 minutes). Pass through a sieve into a small saucepan.

2 For caper butter, bring bonito ichiban dashi to the boil. Remove from heat and add butter, herbs and xanthan gum. Blend with a stick blender until emulsified. Stir in capers, then set aside in a warm place until required.

3 To cook flounder, preheat oven to 200°C. Heat 40ml olive oil in a large cast iron-frying pan over medium-high heat. Add 1 flounder, underside down, and cook, basting with oil, until just golden underneath (2-3 minutes), then transfer to an oven tray. Repeat with remaining olive oil and flounder, then transfer to oven tray. Roast until cooked through (8-10 minutes).

4 To serve, carefully place a flounder onto each plate and spoon over the caper butter. Serve with steamed green beans, a lemon cheek and nasturtium leaves.

NOTE Katsuobushi (bonito flakes) are available at Asian supermarkets. We used a mixture of soft herbs from our kitchen garden, such as little oregano, green shiso, nasturtium, basil and mint.

PREPARE AHEAD Bonito ichiban dashi can be made a day ahead.

WINE MATCH 2019 Valli Waitaki Vineyard Chardonnay, Central Otago.

Braised fennel, stracciatella, pickled cumquats

SERVES 4 // PREP TIME 25 MINS // COOK 45 MINS (PLUS STANDING, PICKLING)

"Fragrant fennel fronds excite the first of your senses," says Cullen. "Then a charred aniseed flavour takes hold, with elegant, creamy stracciatella, followed by the tang of pickled cumquats and strawberry reduction. It's a well-rounded sweet and sour experience from the ingredient combination." You will need to start the recipe two days ahead.

320 gm stracciatella (see note)
4 prosciutto slices
Crusty bread, to serve

PICKLED CUMQUATS
50 gm palm sugar
100 ml rice wine vinegar
100 ml verjuice
250 gm cumquats

STRAWBERRY REDUCTION
80 ml Sherry vinegar
50 gm muscovado sugar
250 gm strawberries, hulled, halved
¼ tsp xanthan gum, optional

BRAISED FENNEL
2 fennel bulbs (about 300gm each), trimmed (see note), fronds reserved, cut into 2cm wedges
1 garlic head, halved crossways
2 thyme sprigs
Thinly peeled rind of 1 lemon
Thinly peeled rind of 1 orange
2 tsp fennel seeds
100 ml extra-virgin olive oil
250 ml fresh apple juice (see note)

1 For pickled cumquats, place palm sugar, rice wine vinegar and verjuice in a small saucepan over medium heat, stirring to dissolve sugar (3-5 minutes). Slice cumquats and discard seeds. Place in a sterilised clean jar, then pour over the pickling liquid. Fill a small bag with water and place on top to submerge cumquats in pickling liquid and seal. Set aside for a minimum of 4 hours or ideally up to 48 hours.

2 For strawberry reduction, place vinegar and sugar in a saucepan over medium heat, bring to the boil, stirring to dissolve sugar. Place strawberries in a small bowl, add vinegar mixture and leave to steep overnight. Place in a high-speed blender and blend, then strain through a fine sieve without applying any pressure (3 hours). Add xanthan gum to thicken slightly if needed and season to taste. Makes 400ml.

3 For braised fennel, preheat oven to 220°C. Place fennel wedges and garlic halves in an ovenproof dish. Scatter with thyme, citrus rinds, fennel seeds and salt to taste, then drizzle with olive oil and apple juice. Cover the surface with a sheet of baking paper, then roast until tender, turning halfway through cooking time and replacing the paper (18-20 minutes).

4 To serve, heat a large, heavy-based frying pan over high heat. Drain fennel from cooking liquid. Pat dry with paper towel, then brown fennel slightly in the pan (1 minute each side). Place 1 tbsp strawberry reduction in each bowl. Add 80gm stracciatella and top with fennel wedges, pickled cumquats, reserved fennel fronds and prosciutto. Serve with crusty bread.

NOTE Stracciatella is available from specialist cheesemakers. If it's unavailable, substitute burrata or mozzarella. If you are making your own apple juice, juice the apple with any fennel trimmings. Leftover strawberry reduction can be used to dress salads. Leftover pickled cumquats can be served with ham and hard cheese.

PREPARE AHEAD Pickled cumquats can be made two days ahead. Strawberry reduction can be made a day ahead.

WINE MATCH 2019 Burn Cottage Riesling Grüner Veltliner, Central Otago.

IN THE
VINES

Delight in distinctive New Zealand terroirs with a tour of some of the finest vineyards in the country. Wander through Marlborough's iconic Cloudy Bay or boutique Rapaura vineyards, discover an epicurean delight at a Havelock North winery or sample a private tasting among the vines at Paroa Bay. With regional, seasonal dining to match, it's a food and wine lover's paradise.

The Shack Cloudy Bay

Discover an epicurean paradise at this contemporary retreat set in Marlborough's most acclaimed vineyard with its world-famous wines, regional dining and unique foraging experiences.

Stay at The Shack Cloudy Bay and you'll soon understand why its award-winning vineyards put Marlborough on the international viticultural map when it was founded in 1985. The Shack not only offers its award-winning wines and regional dining but also unique wine-tasting and foraging experiences.

The Shack takes its name and site from the original bungalow that Cloudy Bay founder, David Hohnen, lived in. Destroyed by fire in 2009, architects Tim Greer and Paul Rolfe designed a new Shack, a modern residence of weathered steel, wood, stone and glass that fits harmoniously with its natural surrounds. The revamped interior features a long dining table burnished in green copper, a floating fireplace and underfloor heating. The distinctly New Zealand interiors feature Kiwiana art and custom local furniture, fittings and materials throughout.

Designed to work harmoniously with its vineyard setting, the property is divided into a comprehensive kitchen, open living spaces and four luxury queen ensuite bedrooms. The Shack is positioned to take in sweeping vistas of the Richmond Ranges, the trademark silhouette that adorns the Cloudy Bay wine label.

Dining at The Shack centres around fresh regional produce used to create the ever-changing seasonal menu at Jack's Raw Bar, the summer garden restaurant popular with locals as well as guests.

While traditional cellar-door tastings are available, guests are invited to explore Cloudy Bay's vineyards, taste the best of local produce, and roll their sleeves up with a number of bespoke experiences. Take a hosted wine tasting and sip on vintages and limited releases from the wine museum with the Tailor Made Tasting experience. Explore the Cloudy Bay terroir by car or by helicopter with the Vineyard Tour. Taste the best of Marlborough region's produce and wines in a seasonal menu prepared by a local chef in the Epicurean Experience. Board a private launch and soak up the natural wonder of the Marlborough Sounds on a luxury 54-foot Beneteau Oceanis yacht.

The rich bounty of the Marlborough region provides plenty of foraging opportunities. The Forage experience sees guests gather wild produce for the chef to transform into a unique season-driven menu. Learn about New Zealand's native flora and fauna while fishing and shucking clams as part of the Sea Forage. The Land Forage takes guests anywhere from Wairau Valley to Marlborough's Pacific Coast depending on the season. Pick herbs, flowers and plants, meet local artisan cheesemakers and sample honey from beehives nestled around the estate's vineyards.

EXPLORE

• Watch the sun set over the vineyard while you relax in the tub with locally made lavender bath salts.

• Stroll through the Pelorus Garden and forage for an array of fresh herbs, fruits and vegetables and create your own gastronomic wonder in The Shack kitchen.

Steamed Cloudy Bay diamond-shell clams with baguette

SERVES 4 AS A STARTER // PREP TIME 20 MINS // COOK 10 MINS (PLUS SOAKING)

"Provenance is all-important, and we are fortunate to have many fantastic local food producers like Cloudy Bay Clams," says chef Sander de Wildt. "There is also something perfect about being able to serve fresh local kai moana, harvested from the area from which we take our name."

2	tbsp extra-virgin olive oil
1	garlic clove, finely chopped
1	golden shallot, finely chopped
1	long red chilli, seeds removed, finely chopped
3	thyme sprigs
1	bay leaf
2	kg Cloudy Bay diamond-shell clams, soaked in cold water for 5 minutes to purge
250	ml Cloudy Bay Sauvignon Blanc
1	large tomato, finely chopped
¾	cup chopped flat-leaf parsley
1	sourdough baguette, warmed Salted butter, to serve

1 Heat olive oil in a large saucepan, preferably with a glass lid, over low heat. Add garlic, shallot, chilli, thyme and bay leaf. Cook, stirring continuously, until just starting to colour (4 minutes). Increase heat to high, add clams and shake the pan for 20 seconds. Add the wine, tomato and half the parsley then cover the pan with a lid. Cook, shaking the pan occasionally (2 minutes). Remove clams from heat as soon as they open, discarding any that remain unopened. Season to taste.

2 Divide clams among bowls, scatter with remaining parsley and serve with warm sourdough baguette and butter for mopping up the cooking juices.

NOTE Since this recipe is such a fast one to execute, if you are entertaining you can have all the elements chopped and ready to go about 4 hours ahead of time.

WINE MATCH 2021 Cloudy Bay Sauvignon Blanc, Marlborough.

Braised beef cheek with porcini, gnocchi and winter greens

SERVES 4 // PREP TIME 1 HR // COOK 9 HRS

"Entertaining at The Shack is all about finding the balance between elegance and relaxation," says de Wildt. "We want our guests to feel at home, and what can be more comforting than the richness and depth of beef cheeks with soft, delicious gnocchi." You will need to start this recipe a day ahead.

40	gm pine nuts, toasted
100	gm Grana Padano, shaved
	Cabbage sprouts, to serve

BEEF CHEEKS

2	tbsp olive oil
4	beef cheeks (800gm)
250	ml pinot noir
1.5	litres beef stock
1	garlic clove, crushed
3	bay leaves
1	rosemary sprig

GNOCCHI

1	kg Agria or Russet Burbank or Nicola potatoes, peeled
1	egg
½	tsp freshly grated nutmeg
225	gm "00" flour or bread flour, plus extra for dusting
	Extra-virgin olive oil, for drizzling
80	gm butter, chopped

PORCINI MUSHROOMS

25	gm dried porcini
60	gm butter
400	gm Swiss brown mushrooms, halved
1	golden shallot, finely chopped
1	tsp thyme leaves
200	gm kale

1 For beef cheeks, heat half the oil in a large frying pan over high heat. Add half the beef cheeks and cook, turning, until browned all over (6 minutes). Transfer to a 5.5-litre slow cooker. Repeat with remaining oil and beef. Add wine, stock, garlic, bay and rosemary to the cooker. Cook, covered, on low or until beef is tender (8 hours). Cool, then remove beef cheeks from liquid, reserving 250ml cooking liquid in the fridge. Simmer remaining cooking liquid until reduced by half (20 minutes). Refrigerate until required.

2 For gnocchi, cook potatoes in a large saucepan of boiling water until tender (35-40 minutes). Drain in a colander and set aside to cool until cool enough to handle (5-10 minutes). Pass through a potato ricer or sieve into a bowl, make a well in the centre and add egg, a pinch of salt, nutmeg and some of the flour. Mix well and keep adding flour until the dough comes together. Add more flour only if the dough feels sticky. Take care not to overwork the dough or this will make the gnocchi tough.

3 Place a large piece of baking paper on a work surface or a large wooden board, dust with extra flour and lightly flatten dough into a rough square, about 1.5cm thick. Cut into 1.5cm-wide strips, using a plastic dough cutter. Dust hands with flour then roll the strips into 1.5cm-diameter cylinders, then cut into 2cm pieces.

4 Cook gnocchi, in two batches, in a large saucepan of simmering water until they float (1-2 minutes). Remove with a slotted spoon and transfer to a tray drizzled generously with olive oil, cover with plastic wrap and refrigerate until required.

5 For porcini mushrooms, soak porcini in a bowl of warm water to soften (15 minutes). Squeeze excess water from porcini, coarsely chop and set aside. Strain soaking liquid and reserve 60ml. Heat half the butter in a large frying pan over medium heat, add enough Swiss brown mushrooms and shallot to just cover the base of the pan and cook, stirring, until well browned (4-6 minutes), then season to taste. Add some of the thyme, chopped porcini and porcini soaking liquid, and cook, stirring, until fragrant. Season, transfer to a tray, then repeat with remaining ingredients. Return all mushrooms to the pan and set aside in the frying pan until required.

6 To serve, preheat oven to 160°C. Portion beef cheeks into large pieces and place in a small ovenproof dish with 250ml reserved braising liquid. Cover with foil and reheat beef cheeks (15 minutes). Meanwhile, heat half the butter in a large frying pan over medium heat. Add half the gnocchi and cook, turning occasionally, until browned (4 minutes). Repeat with remaining butter and gnocchi. Meanwhile, gently reheat mushrooms, add the kale and cook until wilted. Divide beef cheeks among plates, drizzle with reheated reduced cooking sauce, top with mushrooms and gnocchi. Scatter with pine nuts, Grana Padano and cabbage sprouts to serve.

PREPARE AHEAD Beef cheeks can be made up to 2 days ahead.

WINE MATCH 2018 Cloudy Bay Te Wahi Pinot Noir, Central Otago.

Craggy Range

A luxury retreat in the Hawke's Bay's magnificent wine country delivers a food and wine lover's sanctuary with award-winning wines, fine dining and spectacular vineyard and mountain vistas.

A food and wine lover's oasis awaits at Craggy Range nestled in Havelock North's Tukituki River under the majestic escarpment of Te Mata Peak. Immaculate rows of lush green vines are juxtaposed with the stunning mountain vistas to create an idyllic vineyard retreat. World-class wines, fine regional dining and luxury boutique cottages tick all the boxes for the perfect escape.

The four styles of luxury accommodation at the estate's Giants Winery are designed for comfort and privacy. The Craggy Range Lodge perched above the Tukituki Valley offers the ultimate sanctuary with four king bedrooms with ensuites, chef's kitchen, living room with views to Te Mata Peak and dining room with open fireplace. The River Lodges feature two king bedrooms with ensuites, a private courtyard and views of the Tukituki River. The luxurious Garden Cottages offer two king bedrooms with terraces and ensuites, kitchen and living area with wood fireplace and Te Mata Peak vistas. The one- or two-bedroom Vineyard Cottages are set among the vines with kitchen, living area and freestanding wood burners. Cottage breakfast supplies include freshly baked bread, granola, yoghurt and fruit preserves while lodges have continental and cooked breakfast staples.

Craggy Range Restaurant offers relaxed contemporary dining inspired by the finest produce from the Hawke's Bay region as well as its own organic kitchen garden and satellite garden at Tukituki River. For an intimate private dining experience, guests can dine in the quarry cellar or library.

The signature shared menu is a contemporary seasonal offering with wine pairings for each course. Snacks and entrées feature the likes of cured kingfish, horseradish cream, green apple and sorrel sauce; roast haloumi, pine nut sauce, beetroot and burnt honey walnut dressing; and sweet and sour fried shiitake and oyster mushrooms. Mains include slow-roasted lamb shoulder, smoked romesco sauce with pine nut and parmesan crumb served with a side of roast potatoes with confit garlic and a salad of fresh garden greens. Desserts such as citrus cheesecake with rhubarb, lime, white chocolate and almond crumble are based on the freshest fruit of the season.

A stay at Craggy Range would not be complete without a cellar door tasting. Cellar staff expertly guide tastings of the estate's latest releases and discuss the winemaking philosophy of neighbouring vintners in Hawke's Bay, Martinborough and Marlborough. A tour of the winery reveals the Māori legend of the Sleeping Giant, the story of Te Mata Peak after which the Giants Winery is named.

EXPLORE

• Wander through the vineyards and admire the works of New Zealand sculptor Paul Dibble and acclaimed British sculptor Paul Day.

• Discover Craggy Range's winemaking philosophy with the Ultimate Prestige Tasting. Finish with a guided tour of the fermentation cellars and underground barrel hall.

Char-grilled octopus, roasted yams, shaved fennel and hollandaise

SERVES 6 // PREP TIME 40 MINS // COOK 4 HRS (PLUS COOLING)

"This dish combines a delicate balance of the richness of the hollandaise, smokiness of the romesco and sharpness of the bitter cabbage. They work in harmony to dress the octopus," says head chef Casey McDonald.

1 kg tenderised octopus, cleaned
500 gm small yams or kipfler potatoes (see note), peeled
200 ml extra-virgin olive oil, plus extra, for drizzling
1 cup flat-leaf parsley leaves

ROMESCO SAUCE
3 long red chillies
2 red capsicums (250gm each), halved, seeds removed
500 gm ripe roma tomatoes, halved
80 ml extra-virgin olive oil
150 gm crustless sourdough, finely chopped
80 gm blanched almonds
80 gm skinless roasted hazelnuts
4 garlic cloves, crushed
80 ml Sherry vinegar

HOLLANDAISE SAUCE
100 ml white wine vinegar
1 tbsp water
10 white peppercorns
4 egg yolks
Juice of ½ lemon
250 gm clarified butter, at room temperature
Pinch of cayenne pepper

CABBAGE AND FENNEL SALAD
2½ tbsp chardonnay vinegar
1 tbsp Dijon mustard
1 tbsp honey
200 ml blended oil (see note)
100 gm white cabbage, finely shredded
100 gm fennel, thinly sliced
1 tbsp each mint leaves and dill sprigs

1 Preheat oven to 130°C. Grease and line a roasting pan with baking paper and place octopus in pan. Cover with baking paper then cover tightly with foil and cook until tender (2½ hours). Cool then refrigerate until required.

2 For romesco sauce, increase oven to 220°C. Place whole chillies, and capsicum, cut-side up, on an oven tray lined with foil and roast until blistered and blackened (10 minutes). Fold foil over to cover and stand until cool enough to handle (10 minutes), then peel and remove seeds from chillies. Line a second oven tray with foil, place tomatoes, cut-side up, then roast until softened (20 minutes). Cool, then peel and remove seeds.

3 Place yams or potatoes on an oven tray, season to taste and drizzle with oil. Roast with the capsicum and chillies until golden and tender (35 minutes).

4 To finish romesco sauce, heat 1 tbsp olive oil in a frying pan over low-medium heat. Add the sourdough and almonds and cook until golden (5-8 minutes). Place bread, nuts, capsicum, chilli and tomato with remaining romesco ingredients in a food processor. With the motor running, add remaining olive oil in a steady stream until incorporated and smooth with a little texture.

5 For herb oil, blend 200ml olive oil and parsley in a high-speed blender for 3 minutes. Strain through muslin cloth into a bowl.

6 For hollandaise sauce, simmer vinegar, water and peppercorns in a saucepan over medium heat until reduced by one-third (6 minutes), then strain. Place egg yolks in a bowl with lemon juice. Whisk together, then gradually whisk in strained vinegar reduction until an emulsion has formed. Whisk egg mixture in a bowl over a saucepan of simmering water for about 5 minutes until mixture thickens. Slowly add clarified butter a little at a time, whisking vigorously between each addition. Whisk until an emulsion has formed and sauce is thick and forms ribbons (5-10 minutes). Season to taste with salt and cayenne, then set aside and keep warm. (Do not heat the mixture beyond 65°C.)

7 Preheat a lightly greased barbecue or char-grill pan to high. Grill octopus until charred (6-8 minutes).

8 For cabbage and fennel salad, whisk vinegar, mustard and honey in a bowl until combined, then gradually whisk in oil until emulsified. Season to taste. Combine cabbage, fennel, herbs and dressing in a bowl and toss to combine.

9 To serve, cut the octopus into 2cm-thick rounds and divide slices among plates. Place spoonfuls of cabbage and fennel salad, and sliced potato in between octopus as well as spoonfuls of romesco sauce. Place small spoonfuls of hollandaise in the gaps close to each slice of octopus to ensure each bit includes all the components. Dress generously with honey mustard dressing and herb oil.

NOTE We use local yams that are native to New Zealand. The blended oil is a mix of vegetable and olive oils in equal quantities. Leftover romesco sauce will keep refrigerated for a week.

PREPARE AHEAD Octopus can be prepared to the end of step 1 a day ahead. Romesco sauce can be made a day ahead.

WINE MATCH 2019 Craggy Range Gimblett Gravels Les Beaux Cailloux Chardonnay, Hawke's Bay.

Grass-fed beef tartare, tarragon sauce, crisp anchovy

SERVES 4 // PREP TIME 40 MINS // COOK 15 MINS (PLUS COOLING)

"The playfulness of the 'surf and turf' element of this simple dish is what makes it so special," says McDonald. "There is salinity from the anchovy, freshness from the tarragon and great quality beef that all come together for a dish that can be enjoyed with a side of French fries, homemade crisps or charred toast."

400 gm piece beef rump
25 gm tapioca flour (see note)
45 gm can anchovies, drained
Grapeseed oil, for shallow-frying
Tarragon, to garnish
Homemade potato crisps, to serve

TARRAGON SAUCE
150 ml grapeseed oil
1 small golden shallot, thinly sliced
2 garlic cloves, thinly sliced
50 ml white wine vinegar
2 tbsp tarragon leaves
4 hard-boiled egg yolks, cooled
1½ tbsp water

SHALLOT DRESSING
1 small golden shallot, finely chopped
25 gm capers, coarsely chopped
30 ml white wine vinegar
60 ml blended oil (see note)

1 For beef tartare, remove fat and any sinew from beef and discard. Cut beef into 5mm dice. Wrap tightly in plastic wrap and refrigerate in an airtight container until required.
2 For tarragon sauce, heat 40ml oil in a small saucepan over low-medium heat. Cook shallot and garlic until soft (5 minutes). Add vinegar and cook until almost reduced to dry (5 minutes). Cool. Meanwhile, blanch tarragon in a saucepan of boiling water for a few seconds until bright green. Drain and refresh in iced water, then drain again. Place shallot reduction, blanched tarragon and egg yolks in a small food processor and blend, gradually adding the remaining oil, until emulsified (alternatively place ingredients in a jug and blend with a stick blender). Adjust the consistency with water (keeping in mind that it will thicken on standing) and season with salt and more vinegar if needed. Transfer to a piping bag fitted with a small plain nozzle and refrigerate until required. Makes 200ml.
3 For crisp anchovies, place tapioca flour in a bowl. Add anchovies and toss in the flour, shaking off excess. Heat grapeseed oil in a small frying pan over medium heat and, in batches, fry anchovies until golden (4 minutes). Drain on paper towel. Store in an airtight container lined with paper towel until required.
4 For shallot dressing, combine ingredients in a bowl and season to taste. Set aside until required.
5 To serve, combine beef tartare and enough shallot dressing to coat. Spoon tartare among plates and pipe tarragon sauce over the top in random spoonfuls or dots. Top with anchovies and tarragon. Serve with homemade crisps.

NOTE Tapioca flour is available from select supermarkets. The blended oil is a mix of vegetable and olive oils in equal quantities.

PREPARE AHEAD Tarragon sauce and shallot dressing can be made a day ahead.

WINE MATCH 2019 Craggy Range Aroha Te Muna Road Vineyard Pinot Noir, Martinborough.

Tarāpunga & Paroa Bay Winery

Escape to the vineyard at this remote modern luxury residence set in Paroa Bay and surrender to its breathtaking Bay of Islands views, boutique wines and seasonal fine-dining offering.

Perched above a sheltered inlet at Paroa Bay Winery, Tarāpunga villa is one of the few places in the world where you get the sense of the land emerging from the ocean. Enveloped by a peninsula with the iconic Bay of Islands on the horizon, it's easy to see why guests return here year after year for its boutique vineyard, fine dining and luxury villas.

Tarāpunga, one of three villas, named after the local seabirds similarly nestled above the bay, is the epitome of coastal luxury. Overlooking Paroa Bay and the Bay of Islands, the villa's architectural roof pays homage to the soaring wings of its avian namesake. From its meticulously landscaped gardens to the curated artworks on its walls, every aspect of the residence is furnished with the finest attention to detail. With floor-to-ceiling windows for unfettered panoramic views, chef's kitchen, home theatre, heated infinity pool, sauna and tennis court, this residence offers the ultimate retreat. Tarāpunga offers personal chef dining in-villa or dinner at Sage Restaurant.

Fine-dining at Sage Restaurant is inspired by its idyllic setting over the Bay of Islands with moana (ocean) and whenua (land) providing a bounty of seasonal produce. From freshly caught fish in the bay to the produce from local orchards and the onsite kitchen gardens, grown and sourced ingredients combine seamlessly into a refreshing New Zealand take on fine dining. Entrées include te koura mata, a selection of raw and cured New Zealand crayfish, coconut mousse, pickled cucumber, tomato and green onion oil. Mains may include proteins such as Taupō beef grass-fed eye fillet or line-caught Far North snapper fillet. All dishes are thoughtfully matched with wines from the estate's cellar door, so the dining experience provides a holistic full-circle approach.

Paroa Bay Winery vineyard offers guests a boutique winery with only 16,000 vines and varietals including sauvignon blanc, chardonnay, pinot gris, merlot, syrah and malbec using dry-grown viticulture and relying on seasonal cycles. Enjoy a private wine tasting among the vines with a picnic or sample a complimentary wine flight at Sage.

The Bay of Islands is a subtropical region known for its natural beauty and history. With 144 islands between Cape Brett and the Purerua Peninsula, take a boat trip to explore the islands' many scenic walking tracks and beaches. A maritime adventure playground awaits with an abundance of wildlife to discover including penguins, dolphins, marlin, whales and gannets. History buffs can explore the nearby seaside village of Russell (Kororāreka), home to some of New Zealand's most significant historic buildings.

EXPLORE

• Learn about Paroa Bay Winery's varietals from winemaker Paul Goodege while tasting estate wines with a picnic hamper prepared by Sage's kitchen.

• Explore the bounty of the Bay of Islands with a fishing trip with SpotX fishing charters. Catch snapper, kingfish and hāpuku and ask your personal chef to cook your fresh catch for dinner.

Pan-fried snapper, red onion and 'nduja relish, beurre blanc, kawakawa oil

SERVES 4 // PREP TIME 45 MINS // COOK 1½ HRS (PLUS STANDING)

"This dish highlights New Zealand snapper, a quintessential Bay of Islands fish," says executive chef Daniel Fraser. "Kawakawa has been used traditionally as a healing or tonic herb and is still popular for medicinal purposes today. It grows in an abundance around Paroa Bay Winery. In this dish, the leaves have been used to add a peppery element." You will need to start the recipe a day ahead.

4 snapper fillets (about 200gm each), skin on
1 tbsp canola oil
30 gm butter
4 small kale leaves, stems removed
Extra-virgin olive oil, for dressing
Chive flowers, to garnish

KAWAKAWA OIL
100 gm kawakawa leaves (see note)
100 ml extra-virgin olive oil

RED ONION AND 'NDUJA RELISH
50 ml extra-virgin olive oil
500 gm red onions, finely chopped
100 gm passata
1 tbsp Sherry vinegar
50 gm 'nduja
Zest and juice of 1 lemon
2 tbsp finely chopped flat-leaf parsley

ARTICHOKES
2 globe artichokes
Juice of 2 lemons

BEURRE BLANC
125 ml dry white wine
125 ml white wine vinegar
50 gm golden shallot, finely chopped
5 black peppercorns
1 bay leaf
Pinch of dried tarragon
250 ml pouring cream
250 gm cold butter, cut into cubes
60 ml lemon juice

1 For kawakawa oil, blanch kawakawa leaves in a saucepan of boiling water until bright green (30 seconds), then plunge into iced water. Drain and dry well. Blend with oil in a high-speed blender and season to taste. Transfer to a jug and infuse overnight, then strain through a fine sieve or muslin cloth. Makes 100ml.

2 For red onion and 'nduja relish, heat olive oil in a large, heavy-based frying pan over low-medium heat. Add onions and cook, stirring until they begin to soften. Reduce heat to low and cook, stirring frequently, until very soft (30 minutes). Add passata and cook, stirring frequently, until reduced (30 minutes). Stir in vinegar, 'nduja, lemon zest and juice until combined. Season to taste and set aside to cool. Stir in parsley. Makes 330gm.

3 For artichokes, trim artichoke stalks to 2cm, remove tough outer leaves until you reach the pale, tender inner leaves. Using a small sharp knife, trim bases by cutting down the length of the stem to remove the outside of the stalk. Trim 2cm from the top of each artichoke and halve lengthways, then immediately rub cut surfaces with lemon. Scoop out hairy, fibrous choke with a teaspoon and discard. Place artichokes in a large heavy-based saucepan and add remaining lemon juice. Bring to the boil, reduce heat to low, cover and cook until artichoke hearts are just tender (15 minutes). Cool then set aside until required. Cut each artichoke in half again to make eight pieces.

4 For beurre blanc, place wine, vinegar, shallot, peppercorns and herbs in a small saucepan over medium heat and simmer until reduced by half (8 minutes). Strain through a fine sieve and discard solids. Return reduction to a cleaned pan with cream and simmer until thickened (5 minutes). Reduce heat to low, then gradually whisk in butter, one piece at a time, until incorporated. Add lemon juice and season to taste.

5 For snapper, cut four to five horizontal slashes widthways into the snapper skin to prevent it from curling. Season skin with flaked salt. Heat a heavy-based frying pan over high heat, add canola oil, then snapper, skin-side down. Top with baking paper and a heavy pan to weigh it down, and fry until snapper skin is browned and crisp (2-3 minutes), adding a little butter after 1 minute. Turn over, add artichokes and cook for another minute until just browned and warmed. Drain on paper towel.

6 Blanch kale in a saucepan of boiling salted water, drain and toss with olive oil.

7 To serve, arrange snapper, kale, artichokes, red onion and 'nduja relish around a shallow bowl then pour the beurre blanc in the centre. Dot beurre blanc with a little kawakawa oil and garnish with chive flowers.

NOTE Kawakawa (known as bush basil) is a herb endemic to New Zealand. If unavailable, substitute wild onion, chives or parsley.

PREPARE AHEAD Kawakawa oil, red onion and 'nduja relish and artichokes can be made a day ahead.

WINE MATCH 2021 Paroa Bay Rosé, Northland.

Chocolate crémeux, citrus sorbet, pine needle syrup and pine nut brittle

SERVES 8 // PREP TIME 45 MINS // COOK 1 HR 15 MINS (PLUS INFUSING, FREEZING, REFRIGERATION)

"This is a silky dark chocolate mousse with fresh pear, tangy sorbet, crunchy brittle and a fragrant syrup," says Fraser.
"We use Fair Trade chocolate of very high quality, plus citrus and pear grown onsite."

2 beurre Bosc pears, thinly sliced
Micro-fennel, to serve

CITRUS SORBET
500 ml citrus juice (orange, lemon and lime)
250 ml water
100 gm caster sugar
30 gm glucose syrup

PINE NEEDLE SYRUP
100 gm radiata pine needles (see note)
100 gm caster sugar
100 ml water

CHOCOLATE CRÉMEUX
320 ml pouring cream
160 ml milk
4 egg yolks
60 gm glucose syrup
¾ tsp flaked sea salt
225 gm Valrhona Manjari (70% cocoa solids) dark chocolate, finely chopped

PINE NUT BRITTLE
50 gm pine nuts
200 gm caster sugar
300 ml water

1 For citrus sorbet, place juice, water, sugar and glucose syrup in a small saucepan over medium heat and stir until sugar is dissolved (5 minutes). Cool, then churn in an ice-cream machine. Divide sorbet into eight, 60ml holes of a semi-sphere/dome silicone mould then freeze until firm (3 hours). Alternatively, freeze in a container and scoop sorbet to serve.
2 For pine needle syrup, wash, dry and chop the pine needles. Place sugar and water in a small saucepan over medium heat and stir until sugar is dissolved. Add pine needles and simmer gently to infuse (20 minutes). Transfer to a container and chill overnight before straining and storing for later use. Makes 100ml.
3 For chocolate crémeux, place cream and milk in a saucepan over medium heat and bring to a simmer. Remove from the heat. Whisk egg yolks in a bowl with glucose syrup and salt. Gradually whisk in hot cream mixture. Return mixture to pan and cook over low-medium heat, stirring continuously with a wooden spoon, until mixture is thickened slightly and coats the back of the spoon (8 minutes).
4 Pass custard through a fine sieve into a heatproof bowl. Add chocolate and stand until melted (2-3 minutes), then whisk vigorously until smooth. Refrigerate until chilled (2 hours). Transfer crémeux to a piping bag fitted with 1cm plain nozzle and refrigerate until required.
5 For pine nut brittle, preheat oven to 150°C and line an oven tray with baking paper. Place pine nuts on prepared tray and roast until golden (10 minutes). Roughly chop half the pine nuts. Stir water and sugar in a small saucepan over low heat without boiling until sugar dissolves. Increase heat to medium and simmer until a golden caramel. Carefully add chopped and whole pine nuts and a pinch of salt, then pour onto the same lined tray used to cook the pine nuts and spread evenly. Cool, then break into shards. Store in an airtight container in the freezer until required.
6 To serve, place a large ring mould in the centre of each plate, unmould a sorbet in the middle, then pipe chocolate crémeux around sorbet. Remove mould, then place slices of fresh pear and shards of pine nut brittle in the crémeux and garnish with micro-fennel. Pour a little chilled pine needle syrup around the dessert.

NOTE Not all pine needles are edible so ensure that you can identify the variety of pine tree correctly. Alternatively, you can use a rosemary sprig.

PREPARE AHEAD All elements of the recipe can be made a day ahead.

WINE MATCH 2021 Paroa Bay Sauvignon Blanc, Northland.

The Marlborough

While this heavenly retreat in the South Island's wine country recalls its convent past, now it is blessed with a small luxury hotel, boutique vineyard, seasonal dining and the natural wonders of the Marlborough Sounds.

A former convent amid the South Island's Marlborough vineyards is a divine haven for food and wine lovers just 10 minutes' drive from Blenheim airport. Set on 16 acres of prime sauvignon blanc-yielding wine country, The Marlborough is perfectly poised not only for wine lovers but for outdoorsy types looking to explore the Marlborough Sounds.

Originally built in 1901 for the Sisters of Mercy in Blenheim, the two-storey Victorian weatherboard convent was cut into pieces and relocated in 1994 to its current location before a complete overhaul in 2017. The 10-room small luxury hotel is an oasis of calm with its contemporary decor that highlights elements of its history and the large windows throughout that overlook the surrounding vineyards and gardens. As part of the tariff, guests enjoy breakfasts in the Orangery and pre-dinner cocktails and canapés in the Chapel Bar or by the outdoor fireplace.

Harvest's à la carte menu embraces seasonal, local produce grown using sustainable practices, sourced from the region and the property's kitchen garden. Receiving the most sunshine hours in New Zealand, the Marlborough region is not only the country's most prosperous sauvignon blanc region, but also a food bowl of fruits, vegetables, beef, lamb and sustainable seafood, including the hand-speared

butterfish that appears on the menu. The kitchen's Mibrasa charcoal oven lends a unique smokiness to produce in dishes such as charcoal-roasted green shell Mills Bay mussels with kimchi butter and grilled Middlehurst Station lamb rump with potato, peas, mushroom and onion ragù with jus rôti.

The estate produces its own rosé, riesling, malbec, merlot and sauvignon blanc under winemaker Tamra Kelly. Its TM labelled wine is only served at Harvest. Tour the gardens and vineyards to explore more than 500 different types of trees and shrubs, native birds and a meandering creek. Whether you choose to swim in the outdoor heated pool, play a game of tennis or croquet, or watch a cooking masterclass, the hotel has something to suit all tastes.

A visit to The Marlborough must include a day or two exploring the surrounding vineyards and of course the magnificent Marlborough Sounds, only 15 minutes' drive away. Cruise around the sheltered bays and winding waterways of the four distinct sounds of Queen Charlotte, Kenepuru, Pelorus and Mahau to discover its abundant marine life and unique beauty. The 1500 kilometres of pristine coastline from Kaikoura to the tip of d'Urville Island make it a bucket list destination for hiking, kayaking, mountain biking, fishing, swimming with dolphins and whale watching.

EXPLORE

• Tour the property's gardens and vineyards with the gardener to discover the 500 different trees and shrubs and understand the estate's varietals and wine.

• Board a private charter cruise to explore Motuara Island bird sanctuary and then enjoy an onboard lunch of local seafood and Marlborough wines.

Charcoal-cooked green shell mussels with garlic and yoghurt butter, Bandari-spiced crumbs

SERVES 4 // PREP TIME 1 HR // COOK 35 MINS (PLUS PREHEATING BARBECUE)

"This is a deceptively simple-looking dish, with just a few elements coming together," says executive chef Toby Stuart. "Most of the prep can be done in advance, which then leaves the final bit of cooking to be done just before serving. You will need a barbecue with a lid unless you are lucky enough to have a wood-fired oven, which really helps to give the mussels a smoky, sweet flavour."

100   gm unsalted butter
200   gm panko breadcrumbs
1¼   cups coriander leaves, thinly sliced

GARLIC AND YOGHURT BUTTER
500   gm unsalted butter, softened
2   garlic cloves, finely chopped
100   gm Greek-style yoghurt
  Zest and juice of 1 lime

BANDARI SPICE MIX
1½   tbsp cumin seeds
2   tbsp coriander seeds
2   tsp fennel seeds
1   cinnamon quill
2   tsp black peppercorns
1½   tbsp mild curry powder
1¼   tbsp ground turmeric
1   tsp sumac
2   tsp ground ginger

STEAMED MUSSELS
2   tbsp extra-virgin olive oil
½   onion, finely chopped
2   garlic cloves, finely chopped
500   gm leek tops, finely chopped
1   bay leaf, bruised
2.5   kg green-lipped mussels, beards removed, scrubbed (see note)
200   ml dry white wine

1 For garlic and yoghurt butter, process ingredients in a food processor until combined, then transfer to a piping bag fitted with a plain nozzle and refrigerate until required.

2 For Bandari spice mix, place cumin, coriander and fennel seeds in a small non-stick frying pan with cinnamon and peppercorns, dry-roast over medium heat, stirring until fragrant (3 minutes). Add remaining ground spices and stir until fragrant (1 minute). Cool, then blend to a fine powder in a spice grinder. Alternatively, grind with a mortar and pestle. Transfer to a sealed jar and store until required.

3 For steamed mussels, heat olive oil in a saucepan with a tight-fitting lid (preferably glass) over medium-high heat. Add onion, garlic and leek tops and cook, stirring, until softened (8 minutes). Add bay leaf and increase heat to high. Add mussels and wine, cover with a lid and shake pan occasionally until mussels just open (2-3 minutes). Drain mussels into a colander over a small saucepan, then spread out over a tray to cool quickly. Meanwhile, place saucepan of cooking liquid over medium heat and simmer until reduced by half (10 minutes). Check to ensure it's not too salty. Once the mussels are cool enough to handle, remove the mussels and reserve the shells. Using a small knife, remove the small piece of muscle from the shell that was attached to the mussel.

4 For crumbs, melt butter in a non-stick frying pan over low-medium heat. Add breadcrumbs and cook, stirring continuously, until golden brown (4 minutes). Add 30gm Bandari spice mix and stir until combined. Cool, then transfer to an airtight container until required. Makes 3½ cups.

5 To serve, preheat a wood-fired or charcoal barbecue with a lid to at least 300°C. On a tray that fits into the barbecue, place reserved mussel shells and return a mussel, top-side up to each shell. Spoon over a teaspoon of reduced cooking juices, then pipe a teaspoon of garlic and yoghurt butter onto each mussel. Place on the barbecue and cook with the lid down until the butter bubbles and starts to become smoky and the mussels are heated through but not overcooked (3-5 minutes). Arrange mussels among plates, drizzle with cooking juices and scatter generously with Bandari-spiced crumbs. Sprinkle with coriander and season with salt.

NOTE Green-lipped mussels are a large species of mussel only found in New Zealand. Substitute black mussels and adjust quantities slightly for similar results.

PREPARE AHEAD Garlic and yoghurt butter, and Bandari-spiced crumb can be made a day ahead.

WINE MATCH 2021 Neudorf Estate Rosie's Block Moutere Albariño, Nelson.

Grilled red cabbage steak, whipped goat's cheese with herbs, roasted red onion and toasted barley, orange and honey dressing

SERVES 4 // PREP TIME 50 MINS // COOK 3 HRS 5 MINS (PLUS PREHEATING BARBECUE)

"This is a dish with many elements working together to create something that's simple but full of flavour," says Stuart. "We used our Mibrasa charcoal oven to impart a smoky flavour to the cabbage, and it also brings out the sweetness. The goat's cheese adds luxury and the orange dressing helps cut the whole dish and brings all of the flavours together." You will need either a wood-fired oven, charcoal or gas barbecue with a lid for this recipe.

1	large red cabbage (1.5kg)
3	red onions (170gm each), quartered
	Extra-virgin olive oil, for drizzling
1	bunch kale (360gm), trimmed
250	gm pearl barley
500	ml vegetable stock
1	large orange, cut into segments
	Marjoram (or basil) leaves, to serve

ORANGE AND HONEY DRESSING

350	ml freshly squeezed orange juice, strained
2	tsp Dijon mustard
50	ml sweet sherry
1½	tbsp honey
200	ml grapeseed oil

GOAT'S CHEESE AND HERB SAUCE

250	gm fresh goat's cheese, at room temperature
½	small garlic clove, finely chopped
150	gm crème fraîche
1	golden shallot, finely chopped
2	tbsp finely chopped flat-leaf parsley
1	tbsp finely chopped chives

MAPLE GLAZE

100	ml maple syrup
1½	tsp ground Sichuan peppercorns
1	tbsp red wine vinegar
1	tbsp extra-virgin olive oil

1 For cabbage, heat a charcoal barbecue with a lid to 170°C. Trim the base of the cabbage, then remove any poor-quality leaves. Wash and dry cabbage, then wrap tightly in foil. Cook in the barbecue with the lid down or until cabbage is easily pierced with a sharp knife (about 2 hours).

2 Meanwhile, for roasted red onions, drizzle onion quarters with a little olive oil and season. Cook in the barbecue with the cabbage until slightly charred on the edges and cooked through (1 hour).

3 Meanwhile, blanch kale in boiling salted water until tender. Drain and refresh under cold water, then set aside.

4 For toasted barley, place barley in a saucepan over low heat and stir until golden brown (4 minutes). Add stock and a pinch of salt and bring to the boil. Reduce heat to a simmer and cook until it has a bit of bite (10 minutes). Set aside until required.

5 For orange and honey dressing, simmer orange juice in small saucepan over medium heat until reduced to 125ml (14 minutes). Transfer to a blender with mustard, sherry and honey, and blend until combined. With motor running, add oil in a steady stream until emulsified. Season to taste and set side until required. Makes 375ml.

6 For goat's cheese and herb sauce, place goat's cheese, garlic and crème fraîche in a food processor and process until smooth. Transfer to a bowl, stir in shallot and herbs, then season to taste. Refrigerate until required.

7 For maple glaze, place ingredients, except oil, in a small saucepan over medium heat and simmer until reduced slightly (2 minutes). Remove from heat, then whisk in oil. Leave to cool or until required.

8 Once cabbage is cool enough to handle, cut into quarters and place on a tray. Brush with maple glaze. Place on the barbecue grill and cook, turning, until they start to char and colour (2 minutes each side).

9 Combine barley, red onions and kale in a frying pan over medium heat. Cook, stirring occasionally, until warmed through. Season to taste.

10 To serve, divide goat's cheese and herb sauce among plates, spreading into a crescent shape with the back of a spoon. Divide barley mixture and spoon over the goat's cheese. Brush cabbage with remaining maple glaze and place on top of the barley and cheese mixtures. Pour over any remaining juices. Spoon around the orange and honey dressing, and arrange a few orange segments on top. Scatter with marjoram leaves and drizzle with extra-virgin olive oil.

PREPARE AHEAD Orange and honey dressing, and maple glaze can be made a day ahead.

WINE MATCH 2020 Black Estate Home Chenin Blanc, Waipara Valley.

BY THE COAST

Spectacular Pacific Ocean vistas and idyllic island retreats offer a slice of paradise along New Zealand's coastline. Explore private beaches and luxury residences on Purerua Peninsula, coastal farms at Te Awanga and Banks Peninsula, nostalgic Kiwi baches on Waiheke Island, a romantic hideaway in the Bay of Islands and an award-winning wellness sanctuary in Nelson.

The Landing

Tucked away in the Bay of Islands, this idyllic coastal paradise offers privacy in spades with luxury residences, private beaches and its own vineyard and state-of-the-art winery.

Nestled in 1000 acres on the southwestern tip of the Purerua Peninsula in the Bay of Islands, The Landing offers guests an idyllic waterfront haven with its four luxury residences. If exclusivity is what you're after, The Landing, perched on the ocean, also provides guests access to six private beaches.

Accommodation consists of four individual retreats. The five-bedroom Cooper Residence with panoramic views of the Bay of Islands is home to archaeological relics, Māori taonga, historic artefacts and contemporary New Zealand art. The residence also features a wine cellar, tasting room, observation deck and entertainment areas. The Gabriel Residence overlooks Wairoa Bay and sleeps eight with its four king suites, three lounge areas, entertainer's kitchen and multiple outdoor spaces. The Boathouse on the water's edge at Wairoa Bay features a mezzanine master bedroom and twin room downstairs with an outdoor dining space, pizza oven and fire pit perfect for entertaining. The Vineyard Villa overlooks the vines and wetlands and sleeps six guests in its master suite and two king bedrooms.

Apart from its spectacular surrounds and lodgings, The Landing is culturally significant as the neighbouring bay was the site of New Zealand's first township of Māori and European settlers. Developed with the local iwi (Māori tribe) to protect the 43 archaeologically registered sites, The Landing is home to a collection of artefacts and rare books on Northland's and New Zealand's history.

The Landing Wines are known for their depth and complexity as a result of Northland's long, warm summers and coastal aspect. From vine to bottle, every step of the winemaking process takes place on site, starting in the 23-acre vineyard and finishing at the state-of-the-art winery. Guests are taken on a guided tour of the vineyard before a wine-tasting in the sustainable hilltop winery with sweeping views over the property.

For a uniquely personal dining experience, bespoke menus are designed to reflect the garden-to-plate ethos that focuses on The Landing's orchards, vegetable and herb gardens, free-range eggs and fresh catch.

There are many sights and sounds to take in at The Landing. Board The Landing's boat for a tour of the pristine coves and bays, experiencing the marine wildlife as you sail past volcanic rock formations and archaeological discoveries. For a rare opportunity to see New Zealand's iconic native bird up close, be sure to take the guided, late-night kiwi-spotting walk around the property. The kiwi is a very special guest to The Landing and can often be heard foraging in its unique, noisy way.

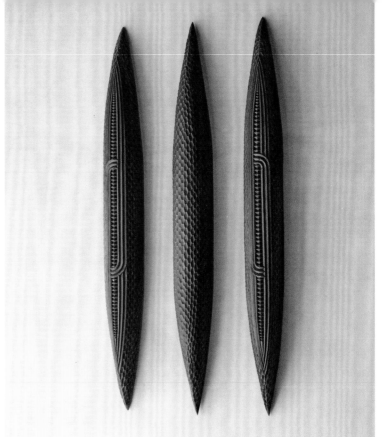

EXPLORE

• Take a short boat trip to award-winning Waitangi Treaty Grounds and Museum to explore 18.5 hectares of native bush, boardwalks, tracks, beaches and coastal clifftops.

• Enjoy pre-dinner sunset drinks at The Landing Winery and soak in the views of the vineyard, native bush and farmland.

Herb-crusted lamb with The Landing Syrah jus and green beans

SERVES 4 // PREP TIME 30 MINS // COOK 1 HR (PLUS RESTING)

This dish is a dinner staple at The Landing, and is best enjoyed with friends and family. Decadent natural flavours infuse the lamb, and the addition of The Landing Syrah adds a unique twist to the classic pairing.

2	French-trimmed 8-cutlet lamb racks
400	gm green beans, blanched
	Snow pea tendrils, to garnish

PARSNIP PURÉE

1	kg parsnips, peeled, cored, cut into 1cm pieces
750	ml milk
750	ml water
4	sage leaves
100	gm butter, chopped

HERB CRUST

6	garlic cloves, finely chopped
15	gm nutritional yeast (see note)
1	firmly packed cup flat-leaf parsley, finely chopped
¼	cup mint leaves, finely chopped
2	tsp finely chopped rosemary
125	ml lightly-flavoured extra-virgin olive oil
2½	tbsp Dijon mustard

THE LANDING SYRAH JUS

1	tbsp grapeseed oil
2	golden shallots, coarsely chopped
175	ml The Landing Port
175	ml The Landing Syrah
1	rosemary sprig
750	ml beef stock
10	gm butter

1 For parsnip purée, place parsnips, 600ml milk, water and sage in a saucepan over medium heat and bring to a simmer. Reduce heat to low and cook until tender (35 minutes). Drain, discarding cooking liquid. Transfer parsnip to a blender and blend with remaining 150ml milk, heated, and butter, until a smooth purée forms. Adjust the consistency with a little extra milk if necessary. Keep warm until required.

2 For herb crust, preheat oven to 180°C. Place garlic, nutritional yeast, parsley, mint, rosemary and 2 tbsp olive oil in a bowl. Season to taste and stir well to combine.

3 Season lamb racks with salt and pepper. Heat remaining oil in a frying pan over medium-high heat. Add lamb and cook on each side until browned all over (3-4 minutes total), then transfer, fat-side up, to an oven tray.

4 Spread mustard over the top of the lamb racks. Divide the herb mixture in two, then spread and pat each portion over the mustard coating on each lamb rack. Roast until cooked to your liking (10-15 minutes for medium-rare, and internal temperature reaches 54°C-58°C on a meat thermometer). Cover loosely with foil and rest (10-15 minutes).

5 Meanwhile, for The Landing Syrah jus, heat oil in a saucepan over medium heat. Add shallots and cook, stirring occasionally, until lightly golden (3-5 minutes). Add port, syrah and rosemary and bring to the boil. Simmer until reduced by half (8 minutes). Add stock and simmer until reduced by half (15 minutes) or until a consistency that will coat the back of a spoon. Remove pan from heat and pass jus through a fine sieve, discarding solids. Return pan to stove and bring to the boil. Remove from heat and whisk in butter, then season to taste.

6 To serve, divide parsnip purée and green beans among plates with halved lamb racks. Spoon around the jus and garnish with snow pea tendrils.

NOTE Nutritional yeast flakes, also known as savoury yeast flakes, are available from select supermarkets and health-food shops.

PREPARE AHEAD Parsnip purée and The Landing Syrah jus can be made a day ahead.

WINE MATCH 2019 The Landing Syrah, Bay of Islands.

Lemon curd tart

SERVES 12 // PREP TIME 40 MINS // COOK 30 MINS (PLUS REFRIGERATION)

This is a summer favourite at The Landing. The tangy flavour and smooth texture of the lemon filling coupled with a buttery and crumbly pastry makes it the perfect sweet treat.

Mint, icing sugar and whipped cream, to serve

PASTRY
250 gm plain flour
55 gm icing sugar, sieved
130 gm unsalted butter, slightly softened
Finely grated zest of 1 lemon
1 tsp lemon juice
1 egg, lightly beaten

FILLING
275 gm caster sugar
185 gm cold unsalted butter, cut into 1cm pieces
Zest of 2 lemons
300 ml lemon juice
5 eggs, lightly beaten

1 For pastry, process flour, icing sugar, butter and lemon zest in a food processor until coarse crumbs form. Add lemon juice and egg, and pulse until pastry dough almost comes together. Form pastry into a 14cm disc, wrap in plastic wrap and refrigerate to firm (1 hour).

2 Roll pastry out on a lightly floured sheet of baking paper until 4mm thick and 35cm round. Place pastry in a 24cm-diameter, 3cm-deep fluted tart tin with removable base, trim pastry and lightly prick base with a fork. Press pastry scraps into a ball and use this to press pastry case into the edges of the tin. Place in the freezer for 10 minutes to rest.

3 Place a heavy-based oven tray in the oven then preheat oven to 160°C. Line pastry case with baking paper, fill with dried rice or dried beans or ceramic pie weights and blind-bake on heated tray for 20 minutes. Carefully remove rice or beans and baking paper and bake for a further 10 minutes or until cooked and golden. Cool.

4 Meanwhile, for filling, heat sugar, butter, lemon zest and juice in the top of a double boiler. Once butter is melted, whisk in the eggs and continue whisking over the heat until the mixture thickens enough to coat the back of a spoon (8-10 minutes). Do not let mixture boil or it will curdle. Remove from heat. Cover surface closely with plastic wrap and leave to cool to room temperature.

5 Fill tart with cooled curd to within 2mm of the top, then bake until just set with a slight wobble (10-15 minutes). Cool tart in tin for 2 hours.

6 Garnish with freshly picked mint. Dust with icing sugar and serve with whipped cream or ice-cream.

NOTE You will need approximately 4 lemons for the amount of juice required for the recipe.

PREPARE AHEAD Lemon curd tart can be made a day ahead.

WINE MATCH 2019 The Landing Chardonnay, Bay of Islands.

The Farm at Cape Kidnappers

Escape to this unique rural retreat with panoramic Pacific Ocean views for the ultimate farmstay experience with its luxury cottage, farm-to-table dining and extraordinary golf course.

Set high atop the cliffs on the southern headland of Hawke's Bay on a 6000-acre working sheep and cattle station, The Farm at Cape Kidnappers offers the ultimate luxury farmland retreat with panoramic views of the Pacific Ocean. The property's headland was named Cape Kidnappers by Captain James Cook, and in Māori is known as Te Kauwae-a-Māui.

The Farm's spacious Hilltop, Hilltop Family, Ridge and Lodge suites by Aspen-based interior designer Linda Bedell exude a sophisticated farm-luxe style. Each of the suites has access to lodge facilities such as the gymnasium, pool, spa and library. For those looking for the ultimate private farmstay experience, the Owner's Cottage is an expansive retreat with four deluxe suites each with its own fireplace, bathroom and private balcony to take in the sweeping views. A large living area with stone fireplace, kitchen, powder room, sitting areas and outdoor jacuzzi complete the palatial package.

The Farm's culinary offering revolves around the produce from its extensive vegetable, fruit and herb gardens. The daily changing menu focuses on fresh seasonal produce from its farm as well as the rich bounty of Hawke's Bay artisan producers. Guests can dine on the all-inclusive breakfast, lunch, pre-dinner drinks, canapés and dinner at myriad locations including the lodge's dining rooms, library, loggia and wine cellar. A private five-course dinner in the lodge wine cellar paired with local Hawke's Bay wines is a special experience for locavores.

Aside from those looking for a rural retreat, The Farm is also a drawcard for golf aficionados for its Tom Doak-designed 18-hole golf course set in the ridge-and-valley landscape. Popular amenities include an outdoor infinity pool, jacuzzi, poolhouse and cabana and gymnasium. The spa facility perched on the hilltop overlooking Hawke's Bay provides the perfect place for relaxation with three treatment rooms and steam showers. For adventures on foot, by mountain bike or 4WD, there's more than 40 kilometres of walking trails to be explored on the property.

The Farm's dramatic landscape encompasses Cape Sanctuary, home to one of the largest mainland gannet colonies in the world, with up to 25,000 gannets in residence between September and May each year. The property offers activities and experiences that draw on the landscape. Whether it's golf, horseback riding, guided birdlife encounters led by the sanctuary team, adventurous Can-Am tours of the property or relaxing spa treatments, guests can choose to do as little or as much as they like.

EXPLORE

• Be sure to book a caddy for invaluable tips and tricks to help navigate your way around Cape Kidnappers' 18-hole course.

• Experience a sunrise at the Black Reef Gannet Colony. Pack a breakfast picnic and witness the morning rituals of nesting gannets from September to May.

Mānuka-smoked kingfish, crème fraîche, braised daikon, pickled lemon

SERVES 4 // PREP TIME 45 MINS // COOK 1½ HRS (PLUS PICKLING)

"This light citrusy entrée suits the hot summer months and pairs effortlessly with white wines," says head chef James Honore. **"It's a regular on summer menus at Cape Kidnappers and features sustainably caught fish and produce from our gardens."**

200	**gm wild rice**
	Rice bran oil, for deep-frying
400	**gm kingfish fillet**
	Mānuka wood chips (see note)
1	**daikon (600gm)**
750	**ml dashi stock (made with 20gm dashi stock powder)**
100	**gm crème fraîche**
1	**pickled jalapeño, finely chopped**
½	**tsp lime zest**
1	**spring onion, finely chopped**
2	**radishes, thinly sliced**
20	**baby mint leaves**
20	**small shiso leaves**

PICKLED LEMONS

3	**small thin-skinned lemons**
100	**gm golden caster sugar**
100	**ml water**
100	**ml chardonnay vinegar**
2	**tsp fine salt**

1 For pickled lemons, wash lemons and slice on a mandolin as thinly as possible, then place in a heatproof bowl. Place sugar, water, vinegar and salt in a saucepan over medium heat and bring to the boil, stirring to dissolve sugar. Pour vinegar mixture over lemons then leave to pickle (4 hours or overnight).

2 For puffed rice, place wild rice in a saucepan of boiling water and cook for 13 minutes or until par-cooked, then drain well. Preheat oven to 80°C. Line an oven tray with baking paper, then spread rice out over the tray. Cook until dehydrated and you can snap a grain (40-60 minutes). Fill a saucepan one-third full with oil and heat to 220°C. Fry rice in small batches (rice will puff instantly), then remove with a mesh spoon to a tray lined with paper towel.

3 For smoked kingfish, pat kingfish dry with paper towel. Remove the blood line from underneath with a small sharp knife. Place a small oiled metal rack in a Dutch oven and place fish on top. Place the end of a smoking gun's hose in the Dutch oven and add a small amount of mānuka wood chips into the burn chamber. Light the wood chips until you see smoke exiting the end of the hose. Cover with a lid and stand for 2-3 minutes. Repeat process five more times, emptying the chamber of wood chips and refilling.

4 For braised daikon, peel and cut daikon into 5mm-thick batons, and place in a saucepan with dashi stock. Bring to the boil over medium heat, then reduce heat to low and simmer gently until daikon is tender but retains some texture (2-3 minutes). Drain and cool.

5 Combine crème fraîche, jalapeño, lime zest and spring onion in a small bowl and season to taste.

6 To serve, place a spoonful of the crème fraîche mixture onto each plate. Cut the kingfish into 5mm-thick slices and place on top. Season with sea salt flakes. Continue layering with drained pickled lemon slices, drained braised daikon, radish, mint and shiso. Scatter with puffed rice.

NOTE Smoking guns are an easy way to cold smoke a variety of foods. They are available online and from specialty kitchen shops and are sold with mānuka wood smoking chips.

PREPARE AHEAD Pickled lemons and braised daikon can be prepared a day ahead. Wild rice can be cooked a day ahead but not fried.

WINE MATCH 2020 Te Mata Cape Crest Sauvignon Blanc, Semillon and Sauvignon Gris, Hawke's Bay.

Thyme-poached apricots, apricot purée, almond cake, malt crumb, goat's cheese sorbet

SERVES 8 // PREP TIME 1 HR // COOK 15 MINS (PLUS FREEZING, COOLING)

"This dessert was created for a winemakers' lunch at the lodge," says Honore. "I love the way the apricots and goat's cheese play off each other, and the interaction between the bee malt crumb, inspired by Christina Tosi's Milk Bar and the bee pollen."

Thyme leaves, and bee pollen (optional; see note), to serve

GOAT'S CHEESE SORBET
- 200 gm caster sugar
- 300 ml water
- Juice ½ lemon
- 400 gm fresh goat's cheese, crumbled
- 250 gm cream cheese, at room temperature

THYME-POACHED APRICOTS
- 1 vanilla bean, split, seeds scraped
- 750 ml water
- 440 gm caster sugar
- 5 wide strips lemon peel
- 2 large thyme sprigs
- 8 apricots, halved and pitted

MALT CRUMB
- 70 gm white chocolate, finely chopped
- 40 gm milk powder
- 40 gm plain flour
- 1 tbsp cornflour
- 25 gm caster sugar
- 50 gm diced butter
- 20 gm malt powder

APRICOT GEL
- 150 ml canned apricot syrup
- ½ tsp agar agar powder (see note)
- 100 gm drained canned apricot halves

ALMOND CAKES
- 4 egg whites
- 35 gm caster sugar
- 25 gm fine almond meal
- 35 gm milk powder
- Cooking oil spray

1 For goat's cheese sorbet, place sugar and water in a saucepan over medium-high heat and stir until sugar dissolves. Bring to the boil and boil for 1 minute, then cool to room temperature. Add lemon juice and refrigerate until chilled (30 minutes). Place goat's cheese and cream cheese in a stand mixer with the paddle attachment and beat until smooth. Add syrup and beat until incorporated. Churn in an ice-cream machine until firm. Sorbet is best used within a day but will keep frozen for up to 1 month.

2 For thyme-poached apricots, add vanilla bean and seeds, water, sugar, peel and thyme sprigs into a saucepan. Bring to the boil, stirring until sugar dissolves. Add apricots and simmer, turning once or twice, or until tender (2-6 minutes).

3 For malt crumb, preheat oven to 140°C. Melt chocolate in a small bowl over a small pan of simmering water, stirring occasionally. Combine milk powder, flour, cornflour, sugar and a pinch of salt in a bowl. Add butter and rub in with your fingers until a sandy consistency. Place on an oven tray and bake until crumbly but not browned (10-15 minutes). Remove from oven, transfer to a bowl and, working quickly, toss through malt powder to coat. Slowly pour in melted chocolate and stir to coat. Spread on an oven tray to cool.

4 For apricot gel, place apricot syrup in a small saucepan over medium heat and bring to the boil. Whisk in agar agar and boil for another 3 minutes. Add apricot halves, cool until thickened, then place in a blender and blend until smooth. Makes ½ cup.

5 For almond cakes, place egg whites and sugar in a bowl and whisk with an electric mixer until soft peaks form. Sift over almond meal and milk powder, then gently fold until just combined. Spray eight 5.5cm x 6cm (base measurement) paper baking cups with spray oil. Divide mixture among cups, taking care not to deflate mixture. Microwave on medium (80% power) until doubled in size (30 seconds). Stand for 3 minutes before inverting onto a wire rack lined with baking paper. (Cakes will rise like a soufflé and deflate a bit.)

6 To serve, place a cake and 2 apricot halves in each bowl. Spoon in malt crumb, a scoop of goat's cheese sorbet, then pipe in a little apricot gel. Garnish with thyme leaves, and bee pollen, if using.

NOTE Bee pollen is food for young honeybees made by worker bees who collect pollen and compress it into tiny pellets to store in the hive. It is available from select health-food shops. Agar agar, a gelling agent derived from seaweed, is available from Asian grocers.

PREPARE AHEAD Goat's cheese sorbet, thyme-poached apricots, malt crumb and apricot gel can be made a day ahead.

WINE MATCH 2013 Paritua Isabella Late Harvest Semillon, Hawke's Bay.

Annandale

Sprawled over a rugged stretch of coastline, this rural retreat
is a tranquil oasis with its luxury villas, sparkling Pacific Ocean vistas,
acres of farmland to explore and seasonal farm-to-table dining.

An hour's drive from Christchurch, the Banks Peninsula's Annandale offers a private oasis with spectacular Pacific Ocean views and acres of farmland to explore. True to its catchcry, "Stay where the world can't find you", Annandale provides a luxury haven where guests can escape the hustle and bustle and immerse themselves in its 4000-acre coastal farm.

Designed by New Zealand architect Andrew Patterson to complement the natural environment, Annandale's luxury villas and historic homestead are an eclectic mix of modern and traditional. Each offers world-class accommodation with an authentic working sheep and cattle farm as its backdrop. Sprawled over 16 kilometres of coastline, each secluded property offers guests the opportunity to disconnect and discover.

The standout property is the historic five-bedroom Annandale Homestead with its ocean vistas, magnificent gardens, restored fernery, infinity pool, spa pool and tennis court. Rustic and charming, the historic Shepherd's Cottage provides a rural retreat for two with uninterrupted views of the vast farmland and the sparkling ocean in the distance. Situated in its own private bay, the luxurious cedar-clad beach house Scrubby Bay offers a magical private setting perfect for a family or group of friends to gather and celebrate with its own private heated lap pool and jacuzzi. For an indulgent romantic escape, the ultra-modern Seascape perched above a bay as if floating over water is the Annandale's crowning jewel. Accessible by helicopter or 4WD, this private oasis with its floor-to-ceiling windows, stone walls and outdoor spa is the ultimate couples' retreat.

The resident chefs at Annandale take a farm-to-table approach as they prepare dishes featuring regional delicacies with produce sourced from Annandale's farm and gardens. Highlights include a seasonal menu showcasing Annandale lamb and beef, vegetables and herbs from the kitchen gardens and fruit from its orchards. Indulge in a private chef dinner in your villa or dine at your leisure with dishes delivered to your villa with last-minute prep instructions.

Guests can choose from a range of activities designed to make the most of the coastal farm. Discover the ins and outs of a working farm with the farm tour; meet the farmer and see his dogs in action rounding up the sheep. Explore the property on foot, by mountain bike or helicopter or take a nature cruise to see Hector's dolphins in the turquoise waters surrounding the property. Flex your culinary muscles with cooking classes run by the kitchen using produce from the farm. And to unwind after a day's activities, relax with a rejuvenating treatment at the spa.

EXPLORE

• From the privacy of your villa, bask in the morning sun rising over the Pacific Ocean and take in the view of the magnificent Kaikōura Ranges.

• Take a guided 4WD tour of Annandale's 4000-acre sheep and cattle farm. Witness the sheep dog muster the flock and go by the shearing shed to watch shearers in action.

Duo of Canterbury quail with scallop mousse

SERVES 4 // PREP TIME 2½ HRS // COOK 50 MINS (PLUS MACERATING)

"The flavour of cherries and citrus marries beautifully with quail while the sweetness of the scallop adds perfect balance," says head chef Rodrigo Marin Rost. "The textural contrast between the vegetables and scallops makes for a real dining sensation."

4	quails (160gm each)
1	tbsp vegetable oil
2	tbsp honey
30	gm butter
4	large scallops, roe removed
	Pearl barley, roasted
	Diced roasted carrots and micro herbs, to serve

SCALLOP MOUSSE

50	gm scallop meat, roe removed
½	tsp finely chopped flat-leaf parsley
½	tsp lemon zest
1	tbsp pouring cream

QUAIL LEG LOLLIPOPS

1	egg
½	tsp Dijon mustard
2	tbsp plain flour
40	gm panko breadcrumbs
500	ml vegetable oil

CARROT ORANGE PURÉE

500	gm carrots, peeled and diced
350	ml orange juice
100	ml vegetable stock

MACERATED CHERRIES

250	gm fresh or frozen pitted cherries
20	gm caster sugar
1	juniper berry, crushed
1	tbsp lemon juice

CITRUS JUS

	Zest and juice of 1 lemon, 1 orange and 1 lime
1	star anise
125	ml beef jus
80	gm caster sugar
10	gm butter
¼	tsp raspberry vinegar

1 To remove breasts from quail, run a knife along either side of the breast bone, then holding the knife at a slight angle, work the knife along the rib cage to release with the wing bone attached. Repeat on the other side of the quail, then with remaining quail. You will have 8 quail breasts with wing bone attached. Scrape meat from wing bones with a small knife, then French-trim the end of the wing. Season quail breasts all over then stack 2 breasts together, flesh-side to flesh-side. Remove one of the wing bones from each stack so that each resembles a large quail breast. Wrap stacks tightly in plastic wrap and refrigerate (2 hours) so the pieces stay together during cooking.

2 Meanwhile, for scallop mousse, pulse scallops in a food processor until smooth. Add ¼ tsp salt, pinch of white pepper, parsley and lemon zest, and mix briefly to combine. Add cream and pulse briefly just to combine, taking care not to overmix or the mixture will split. Transfer mousse to a piping bag fitted with a plain nozzle and place in the fridge until required.

3 For quail leg lollipops, remove thigh bone from thighs then clean the leg bone, scraping off the meat with a small knife, while retaining as much of the skin around the leg as possible. Place a leg, skin-side down, on a piece of plastic wrap. Pipe scallop mousse over thigh flesh, leaving a small border. Then, using plastic wrap, twist to form a tight ball and secure with kitchen string. Place in the freezer to firm (30 minutes).

4 For carrot orange purée, place ingredients and salt to taste in a large saucepan over low heat. Cook, covered, until very tender (15-20 minutes). Uncover and cook until liquid is nearly evaporated (8-10 minutes). Blend carrot and remaining liquid in a high-speed blender until smooth. Return to the pan and keep warm.

5 For macerated cherries, place ingredients in a bowl. Set aside, stirring occasionally.

6 For citrus jus, place juices, star anise and beef jus in a jug. Place sugar in a saucepan over medium heat. Cook, swirling the pan until sugar dissolves to a deep amber colour. Working quickly, add juice mixture to arrest cooking, then simmer until reduced by three quarters and syrupy. Add zests, butter and vinegar, then season.

7 To cook quail breasts, carefully unwrap. Heat oil in a frying pan over low-medium heat. Add quail, wing-side down, and cook until golden brown (3-4 minutes each side). Add honey to pan and spoon over quail to glaze. Drain quail on a paper towel.

8 To cook quail leg lollipops, lightly beat egg with mustard in a bowl. Place flour in a separate bowl and season. Place breadcrumbs in a third bowl. Unwrap quail lollipops, dust each in flour, dip in egg, then coat in breadcrumbs, shaking off the excess. Heat oil in a large saucepan to 175°C. Add quail and cook until golden (2-3 minutes). Drain on paper towel and season with salt.

9 Heat butter in a small frying pan over medium-high heat. Season scallops with salt, then cook until golden (30-45 seconds each side).

10 To serve, spoon barley onto plates and top with a quail breast. Add quail lollipop, scallop, roast carrot, carrot orange purée, cherries and micro herbs.

WINE MATCH 2019 Greystone Vineyard Ferment Pinot Noir, North Canterbury.

White chocolate and yoghurt ganache, honey panna cotta, honey crémeux, bee pollen, kiwifruit, elderflower gel and matcha powder

SERVES 8 // PREP TIME 30 MINS // COOK 15 MINS (PLUS SETTING)

"The combination of white chocolate, crunchy bee pollen and honey is becoming one of the favourites among our guests at Annandale," says Marin Rost. "The ganache is made with Greek yoghurt, giving it the lightest texture and making it a fantastic dessert for any occasion and a variety of palates."

4 gold kiwifruit, peeled
1 tsp bee pollen (see note)
Matcha powder (see note),
for dusting

WHITE CHOCOLATE GANACHE
120 ml pouring cream
225 gm white chocolate
180 gm Greek-style yoghurt

HONEY PANNA COTTA
1½ titanium-strength gelatine leaves
125 ml milk
125 ml pouring cream
90 gm mānuka honey
½ vanilla bean

HONEY CRÉMEUX
2 titanium-strength gelatine leaves
6 egg yolks
70 gm granulated sugar
115 gm mānuka honey
500 ml pouring cream
1 tsp fine salt

ELDERFLOWER GEL
175 ml elderflower cordial
325 ml water
5 gm agar agar powder (see note)

1 For white chocolate ganache, place cream in a small saucepan and bring almost to the boil. Place chocolate in a small bowl and pour over hot cream mixture, and whisk until smooth and melted. Add yoghurt and using a stick blender, mix until just combined. Transfer to a container and refrigerate until set (1 hour). Spoon into a piping bag.

2 For honey panna cotta, soak gelatine leaves in a bowl of cold water until softened (3-5 minutes). Place milk, cream, honey and vanilla in a saucepan and bring to a simmer (see note). Squeeze excess water from gelatine, add to the cream mixture and stir until dissolved. Strain through a sieve and pour into four 100ml plastic dariole moulds and refrigerate until set (2 hours or overnight).

3 For honey crémeux, soak gelatine leaves in a bowl of cold water until softened (3 minutes). Squeeze out excess water and set aside. Whisk yolks and sugar in a bowl until smooth. Heat honey in a saucepan over medium heat until a dark amber colour (2-3 minutes). Bring cream almost to the boil in a small saucepan and slowly whisk into honey. Whisk honey and cream mixture into egg mixture until combined, then return mixture to cream saucepan. Cook over medium heat, stirring continuously until mixture thickens enough to coat the back of a spoon or reaches 81°C. Remove from heat, stir in softened gelatine and salt until dissolved. Refrigerate until chilled (2-3 hours). Whisk until smooth, then place in a piping bag.

4 For elderflower gel, place elderflower cordial, water and agar agar in a small saucepan over medium heat and whisk continuously until mixture boils and thickens (2 minutes). Pour into a container and refrigerate until required.

5 For kiwifruit discs, cut kiwi into 1cm-thick rounds, then cut out the centre of half with a 2-3cm cutter. Reserve all kiwi shapes.

6 To serve, turn out panna cottas and cut in half. Place a panna cotta half in the centre of each plate, pipe three large rounds of chocolate ganache onto each plate. Arrange kiwifruit rings and cut-outs, then pipe honey crémeux. Place a little bee pollen on the plate, dust the crémeux with matcha powder and add spoonfuls of elderflower gel.

NOTE Bee pollen is food for young honeybees made by worker bees who collect pollen and compress it into tiny pellets to store in the hive. It is available from health-food shops. Matcha, a Japanese powdered tea, is available from health-food and tea shops. For panna cotta, ensure mixture doesn't boil or it will split. Agar agar, a gelling agent derived from seaweed, is available from Asian grocers.

PREPARE AHEAD All elements of the recipe can be prepared a day ahead.

WINE MATCH 2020 Pegasus Bay Aria Late Picked Riesling, Waipara Valley.

The Boatshed

Recalling nostalgic New Zealand beach holidays, this luxury boutique hotel on Waiheke Island is the ultimate escape with its stylish bach-inspired villas, idyllic beaches and relaxed island pace.

Nothing says remote luxury quite like The Boatshed, a boutique hotel on the small island of Waiheke, a 35-minute ferry ride from Auckland. If an island getaway is on your radar, The Boatshed is sure to tick all the boxes for sand-between-your-toes luxury with its chic suites, pristine beaches, vineyards and alfresco dining.

Whether you arrive on Waiheke by boat, plane or helicopter there is nothing like an island escape for its relaxed pace and charm. Situated above Oneroa Beach, The Boatshed not only offers luxury digs with bay views but also alfresco dining options and places to unwind and explore.

This family-owned property was developed by New Zealand designer David Scott as the perfect beach retreat. The bach, a New Zealand term used to describe small holiday beach shacks, is the inspiration for the relaxed coastal vibe of The Boatshed's accommodation. The guest rooms feature king-size beds, sea views and open fireplaces in a nostalgic beach-hut style. The Bridge with its nautical ship-inspired interiors overlooks the beach. The three-storey Lighthouse with its spiral staircase and white-washed interiors offers an idyllic romantic honeymoon escape. The zinc-clad Watertower is a modern storeyed villa with views on three sides. The Bungalows are classic

bach reinvented. For the ultimate beach holiday escape, the two-bedroom Owner's Cottage features a chef's kitchen, multiple dining and living areas, fireplaces, a private pool and a grand piano.

The chef and gardener work closely to grow seasonal produce in the kitchen gardens to highlight the best New Zealand has to offer from the farm to the sea. The fresh, seasonal menu is centred around the gardens' organic produce and is only available to in-house guests. Dining tables are discreetly set around the property for guest comfort and privacy.

The relaxed island pace at The Boatshed means that guests can choose to do very little; relax with a great book, enjoy a lazy breakfast, book a massage in the spa or stroll on the beach. Those looking to explore won't be disappointed; from vineyards and beautiful coastal walks to paddle boarding and kayaking, everyone's tastes are catered for.

Swimming at Waiheke, in little coves and bays to long sandy beaches, is a highlight. A coastal walkway system allows for spectacular hiking; take a 40-minute walk around the headland or a 4-hour hike. Aside from these activities, Waiheke's sophisticated vineyard restaurants, vibrant village and market, established and emerging artist studios all offer guests so much to see, taste and enjoy.

EXPLORE

• Hit the northern road down the island in a Boatshed Picnic Truck. Explore beaches and the off-the-beaten-track Man O' War loop. Roll out the jeep's awning to enjoy a pre-packed lunch before heading back along the southern side of the island.

• Start your day with morning yoga on the beach and a walk to Fisherman's Rock before heading back for breakfast overlooking the bay.

Crisp-skinned snapper with clams and saffron broth

SERVES 6 // PREP TIME 40 MINS // COOK 25 MINS (PLUS SOAKING)

"Snapper is in abundance in the Hauraki Gulf, and we love to use it whenever we can," says The Boatshed manager Jonathan Scott. "The lightness of the broth, the richness of the clams, the flavour and colour of the saffron, and the aniseed of the fennel, set it off – this simple gremolata is a kitchen staple!"

80	ml extra-virgin olive oil
3	golden shallots, finely chopped
2	garlic cloves, finely chopped
600	gm clams, scrubbed, purged
18	medium green prawns (400gm), peeled, deveined, leaving tails intact
250	ml dry white wine
	Pinch of saffron threads
3	fennel bulbs (200gm each), halved or quartered, depending on size
500	ml fish stock
1	tbsp Pernod
6	snapper fillets (about 170gm each), skin-on
	Warmed bread, to serve

GREMOLATA

½	cup each finely chopped curly leaf- and flat-leaf parsley
1	garlic clove, finely chopped
	Zest of 1 lemon
2	tbsp finely chopped preserved lemon
125	ml extra-virgin olive oil

1 For gremolata, combine ingredients in a small bowl and set aside until required. Makes 200ml.

2 Heat a large, heavy-based saucepan over medium heat. Add 2 tbsp oil, shallots and garlic, and cook, stirring occasionally, until softened (4 minutes). Add clams and prawns, and cook, turning, until clams just open (1-2 minutes). Remove clams and prawns and set aside. Add wine and saffron to the pan, simmer until reduced by half (3-4 minutes). Add fennel bulbs, cut-side down, pour over fish stock and cover with a cartouche. Simmer until fennel is tender, turning halfway through cooking time (10-12 minutes). Add Pernod then season to taste. Set aside.

3 Score two to three slashes into the skin of the snapper fillets with a sharp knife, pat fish dry and season. Heat remaining oil in a non-stick frying pan over medium-high heat and cook snapper, skin-side down, until skin is crisp (2 minutes). Turn the fillets over and remove from the heat. Set aside for the residual heat of the pan to finish cooking the fillets through without overcooking.

4 Return the broth over a medium heat until heated through. Add the prawns and clams and cook until warmed through (2 minutes).

5 To serve, ladle fennel, clams and prawns among bowls, then ladle over the broth. Top each bowl with a snapper fillet and spoon over the remaining broth. Add a little gremolata and serve with warmed bread.

WINE MATCH 2019 Sam Harrop Onetangi Chardonnay, Waiheke Island.

Salt-roasted garden beetroots with honey-baked goat's cheese

SERVES 6 // PREP TIME 1 HR 15 MINS // COOK 1 HR 5 MINS (PLUS REFRIGERATION, STANDING)

"This is a dish that we love. The hotel's gardens are always abundant with earthy beets, and, combined with creamy chèvre and locally sourced mānuka honey, this makes for a simple and satisfying starter," says Scott.

2	kg assorted coloured beetroot (see note)
200	gm walnut halves
90	gm mānuka honey
600	gm fresh goat's cheese
1	bunch watercress, sprigs picked
	Extra-virgin olive oil

SALT CRUST

250	gm plain flour
400	gm sea salt
2	egg whites
1	tbsp finely chopped rosemary
150	ml water

DRESSING

1	tsp Dijon mustard
2	tbsp chardonnay vinegar
1	tbsp lemon juice
60	ml extra-virgin olive oil

1 For salt crust, place flour, salt, egg whites and rosemary in a food processor. With the motor running, gradually add water until a firm, but not sticky, dough forms. Turn out onto a bench and shape into a ball. Cover and refrigerate until firm (30 minutes).

2 Pick and reserve any small pretty beetroot leaves, then trim tops and scrub beets, leaving them unpeeled.

3 Preheat oven to 180°C. Line an oven tray that holds the beets snugly with baking paper. Roll out the salt crust until it is large enough to cover the beets on the tray. Place it over the beets, then press around each one so they are well covered with the salt crust. Bake until a knife slides through without resistance (60 minutes or more if you are using large beetroot). Set aside to cool.

4 Meanwhile, place walnuts on a small oven tray lined with baking paper and drizzle with 30gm honey. Place tray in the oven and roast alongside the beets and cook, stirring once or twice, to coat in honey or until golden (10 minutes).

5 Crack the salt crust and rub the skin off the beetroots, then cut into slices and thin wedges, keeping each colour separate so the colours do not bleed together.

6 Divide goat's cheese into six evenly sized balls, then create a well in the top of each ball. Fill each with 1 rounded tsp honey. Refrigerate until required.

7 For dressing, whisk mustard, vinegar and lemon juice together in a small bowl, then whisk in oil until combined. Season to taste. Set aside until required.

8 To serve, heat an oven grill to high. Place goat's cheese balls on a greased oven tray and position under the grill close to the element. Grill until honey chars and cheese softens slightly (2-3 minutes).

9 To serve, arrange an assortment of beets on each plate. Using a palette knife, lift and place each cheese portion in the middle. Arrange walnuts, watercress and beet leaves around, then spoon over the dressing.

NOTE We used 2 bunches (2kg) each red and golden baby beets. You can use any combination of golden, red or target beetroot, or focus on a single colour for this recipe.

PREPARE AHEAD Beetroot can be cooked a day ahead. Dressing can be made a day ahead.

WINE MATCH 2021 Mudbrick Rosé, Waiheke Island.

Helena Bay Lodge

Seduce the senses with a romantic escape at this retreat just south of the Bay of Islands, enjoying Pacific Ocean views, pristine beaches, Italian-inspired estate-to-plate dining and an impressive wine cellar.

A secluded retreat in the northeast corner of New Zealand's North Island, Helena Bay Lodge with its pristine stretch of coastline and private beaches, is the ultimate romantic escape. Its picturesque coastal setting and spectacular Pacific Ocean views make it the perfect place for an intimate getaway.

Accommodation includes five luxury suites with balconies overlooking Helena Bay beach and the South Pacific Ocean. Each suite is provided with Leica binoculars for spotting birdlife, whales and dolphins. Guests are welcome to explore the main house with its eclectic artwork and treasures collected by the owners during their travels. Facilities include a gymnasium, sauna, massage room, 25-metre heated swimming pool, library, lounge areas, informal and formal dining areas and an outdoor fire pit.

Dining is informed by the Italian Michelin-starred Ristorante Don Alfonso 1890. Don Alfonso's philosophy of respecting local produce while incorporating the traditions of the Sorrento peninsula and Amalfi Coast defines fine dining at Helena Bay. While the daily changing menu reflects Don Alfonso's philosophy, the kitchen creates estate-to-plate dining using fresh produce from its farm and gardens. Both the three-course and five-course dégustation dinner menus highlight the kitchen's signature dishes.

Whether you choose an elegant candlelit dinner by one of the fireplaces or on the terrace overlooking the Pacific, there are plenty of romantic options. Poolside lunches or a picnic on one of the private beaches are also available.

The wine cellar holds more than 2500 bottles of carefully selected New Zealand and international wines with 300 selections. The wine manager can expertly match the perfect wine companion for the seasonal dishes served in the many dining venues.

Situated in a secluded bay, Helena Bay Lodge is ideally located to provide easy access to the Bay of Islands and Poor Knights Islands which have been shortlisted as a UNESCO World Heritage site. These islands feature the world's largest sea cave and are populated by orca, dolphins and hundreds of fish species. Diving is popular here and is rated among the best in the world.

Guests at Helena Bay can choose from a range of activities including claybird shooting, paddleboarding, kayaking, tennis, mountain biking and fishing. Those interested in exploring the estate's verdant grounds can take a walk along its 15 kilometres of hiking trails. Or indulge in the ultimate sightseeing tour with a scenic flight in the lodge's AgustaWestland helicopter before ending the day with a relaxing spa treatment.

EXPLORE

• Book the beach pavilion for a private alfresco lunch. Make a dramatic entrance by kayak around the coast or use one of the lodge's electric buggies.

• Hook your own dinner off the lodge's luxury charter boat or from the jetty in front of the lodge, then ask the chefs to prepare a true ocean-to-plate dish.

Spaghetti aglio, olio e peperoncino, crayfish tartare, caviar

SERVES 4-6 // PREP TIME 30 MINS // COOK 25 MINS

"This iconic Italian pasta dish is always on our menu," says head chef Michele Martino. **"It is a typical Neapolitan recipe, part of the range of cucina povera, or 'poor' recipes of Neapolitan cuisine. The combination of fresh local crayfish, caught off the Helena Bay coast, and the crunchiness of breadcrumbs paired with Russian sturgeon caviar, makes every bite a delight."**

CRAYFISH TARTARE

200	gm sashimi-quality crayfish tail, (cleaned and cut in 1cm cubes; see note)
1	tbsp extra-virgin olive oil
	Zest of 1 lemon
	Flaky sea salt, to taste
	Watercress sprig, to garnish

BREADCRUMBS

½	garlic clove
2	anchovy fillets
1	tsp capers
1	tbsp extra-virgin olive oil
75	gm panko breadcrumbs
	Zest of ½ lemon

PASTA

320	gm bronze-cut spaghetti (see note)
100	ml extra-virgin olive oil
2	garlic cloves, finely chopped
	Chilli flakes, to taste
1	garlic clove, crushed
1	tbsp finely chopped flat-leaf parsley
1½	tbsp sturgeon caviar (7gm)

1 For crayfish tartare, combine crayfish, olive oil, lemon zest and sea salt to taste in a bowl.

2 For breadcrumbs, finely chop garlic, anchovies and capers together. Heat olive oil in a frying pan over medium heat. Add the chopped ingredients and cook until fragrant (1 minute). Add breadcrumbs and cook, tossing until golden brown (8-10 minutes). Remove from heat and stir in lemon zest. Cool, then transfer to an airtight container until required.

3 For pasta, bring 3 litres of salted water to the boil in a large saucepan. Add pasta and cook a little less than al dente (about 6 minutes). Meanwhile, heat half of the olive oil in a deep frying pan over low-medium heat. Add finely chopped garlic and chilli and cook for 1-2 minutes. Just before the garlic is about to colour, add 60ml pasta cooking water to the pan (or as desired). Increase heat to high and simmer until the water is reduced by half (2 minutes). Drain the pasta, reserving 300ml water. Add pasta to the frying pan and stir vigorously as it continues to cook. Add reserved pasta water, a little at a time as necessary to finish cooking the pasta and develop the thickened sauce. In the final 2 minutes of the cooking process, add crushed garlic, chopped parsley and remaining olive oil. Stir to combine and season to taste.

4 To serve, divide the marinated crayfish among plates. Using a carving fork, twist the spaghetti in a ladle to form a round shape, then place over the crayfish. Sprinkle with breadcrumbs and top with a quenelle of caviar. Garnish with watercress.

NOTE If you are unable to source crayfish, scallops make an excellent substitute. Pasta that is extruded through bronze dies as opposed to plastic. It has a coarser exterior that helps the sauce adhere to it better and is recommended here.

PREPARE AHEAD Breadcrumbs can be made 4 hours ahead.

WINE MATCH 2019 Prophet's Rock Pinot Gris, Central Otago.

Grandfather hāpuku, acqua pazza-style

SERVES 4 // PREP TIME 40 MINS // COOK 30 MINS

"Acqua pazza, meaning 'crazy water', was invented by Italian fishermen in a time when salt was particularly expensive, so they began to stew fish in seawater, along with other simple ingredients like tomatoes, garlic and parsley," says Martino. "We reclaimed this traditional recipe for modern cuisine. Scorpion fish is one of New Zealand's rarer catches, but it convinces with flavour, colour and texture."

500 gm diamond-shell clams (see note), soaked in cold water for 30 minutes
800 gm grandfather hāpuku (scorpion fish), skin-on, cut into 4 portions (see note)
      Baby basil leaves, to serve

ACQUA PAZZA-STYLE FISH BROTH
1½ tbsp extra-virgin olive oil
1 garlic clove, finely chopped
2 tsp small capers
6 anchovy fillets
40 gm tomato passata
600 ml fish stock
      Sea salt and chilli flakes

VEGETABLE BRUNOISE
1 zucchini (120gm)
1 yellow capsicum (200gm)
1 golden shallot
2 tbsp extra-virgin olive oil
      Chilli flakes, to season

1 For acqua pazza-style fish broth, heat olive oil in a wide saucepan over low heat. Add garlic, capers and anchovies, and cook until fragrant (2 minutes). Add passata and fish stock, and simmer until reduced by half (10 minutes). Season with salt and chilli flakes.

2 For vegetable brunoise, cut vegetables into 5mm cubes. Heat olive oil in a frying pan over medium heat and cook vegetables until softened slightly and zucchini is still bright green (3 minutes), then season with chilli flakes. Set aside until required.

3 Transfer 250ml acqua pazza-style fish broth into a saucepan. Add clams and cook, covered, over medium heat, shaking the pan occasionally until the clams open (3-5 minutes). Remove clams from broth, then remove clam meat from the shells and set aside.

4 Strain the clam cooking liquid into the remaining acqua pazza-style fish broth and bring to a gentle simmer over low-medium heat. Add fish, skin-side up, to the liquid in a single layer and cover with a cartouche. Cook until the fish is just starting to flake on the outside (6-8 minutes depending on the thickness of the fish).

5 Remove the fish from the poaching liquid and divide among bowls with the clam meat. Strain the cooking liquid into a jug and pour among the bowls. Top fish with a little of the vegetable brunoise and garnish with baby basil leaves.

NOTE Diamond-shell clams are prized for their high meat-to-shell ratio. Substitute red emperor, blue-eye trevalla or snapper for hāpuku.

PREPARE AHEAD Acqua pazza-style fish broth can be made a day ahead.

WINE MATCH 2013 Hanz Herzog Nebbiolo, Marlborough.

Split Apple Retreat

Check in to this intimate sanctuary at the edge of Abel Tasman National Park and surrender body and soul to its award-winning wellness treatments and Asian-Mediterranean fusion dining.

S tanding at the gateway of Abel Tasman National Park on New Zealand's South Island, Split Apple Retreat is a drawcard for its internationally recognised wellness treatments, creative dining and enviable location. With unparalleled Tasman Bay views, Split Apple offers an intimate retreat where guests can disconnect and unwind in its tranquil natural surrounds.

Owned by hosts Lee Nelson and Anne Pen Lee, the multi-level retreat offers guests a deluxe wellness haven with Asian-inspired interiors, spa treatments, gourmet healthy meals and even a Japanese onsen and garden. Accommodation reflects the intimate scale of the retreat with three luxurious suites each with panoramic views of Abel Tasman National Park and the Tasman Bay. The Lotus and Fuji are oceanfront Japanese-style suites with super-king and king beds respectively, Japanese granite baths and two private balconies and fragrant gardens. The Rainbow is a split-level oceanfront suite with super-king and sofa bed, private decks and Western-style bath.

Wellness treatments are an integral part of the Split Apple Retreat experience and hosts Nelson, a retired doctor, and Pen Lee, the retreat's chef, work together with guests to design a personal wellness itinerary with spa and wellness treatments to complement the fresh, healthy cuisine.

Dining at Split Apple is more than just a culinary experience, it's instrumental to the health and wellness journey at the retreat. The chef's Asian-Mediterranean fusion menu uses the freshest produce organically grown on its sister property Golden Bay or sourced from local producers. Mindfully created, each dish is a blend of ingredients chosen for their health benefits. An extensive wine cellar showcases the best of New Zealand, Australia, France, Germany, Italy and more.

A range of wellness services and facilities help guests achieve optimum health during their stay. Take a rejuvenating dip in the outdoor Japanese onsen or saltwater infinity pool with views of the Abel Tasman National Park and Tasman Bay. Unwind and revitalise in the infrared sauna or steam room. Boost your immune system with therapeutic massage treatments including reiki, acupuncture, reflexology and Thai massage. Learn the ancient art of meditation in a custom theatre using the latest high-tech brain entertainment methods. Improve flexibility with yoga lessons in the Yoga Pavilion.

If time permits, explore the impressive walking tracks of Abel Tasman National Park or discover the retreat's namesake, the 120-million-year-old Split Apple Rock, with private guest access leading to the beach.

EXPLORE

• Look out for the native little blue penguins who nest on the retreat's grounds each year.

• Try a healing and rebalancing reiki treatment or an invigorating Thai massage by the retreat's highly skilled therapists.

LARB PLA

Ceviche, Thai-style

SERVES 2 // PREP TIME 25 MINS // COOK 10 MINS (PLUS MARINATING, COOLING)

"Thai ceviche is a celebration of raw, marinated fish with spices and herbs chosen to balance the flavours, and lime juice to enhance the sour taste of the fish," says chef Anne Pen Lee. "The freshness from herbs like lemongrass, mint and coriander helps to soothe indigestion and stomach issues while naturally boosting immunity. They're good for your heart, brain and skin, too."

300 gm white fish or snapper fillet
 (see note)
 80 ml lime juice
 1 tsp sea salt
 1 tsp chilli flakes
 2 red shallots, thinly sliced crossways
 1 tbsp soy sauce
 Juice of 1 lemon
 1 spring onion, thinly sliced
 1 lemongrass stalk, white part only,
 very thinly sliced
 ¼ cup coriander leaves, chopped,
 plus extra to serve

TOASTED RICE POWDER
 70 gm uncooked glutinous rice
 2 makrut lime leaves
 1 lemongrass stalk, white part only,
 thinly sliced

1 Cut fish into 1.5cm cubes and place in a bowl. Drizzle over lime juice and sprinkle with salt. Mix well, then cover and refrigerate for flavours to permeate (a maximum of 30 minutes).

2 Meanwhile, for toasted rice powder, place rice, makrut lime leaves and lemongrass in a dry frying pan over medium heat. Stir continuously until the rice begins to brown and lime leaves and lemongrass are dry and crisp (about 5-7 minutes). Set aside to cool. Place rice mixture in an electric spice grinder or coffee blender and grind to a gritty powder (like coffee grounds). Transfer to an airtight jar and store until required, or for up to 1 month.

3 Meanwhile, for the chilli sauce mixture, place chilli flakes, shallots, soy sauce, lemon juice, spring onion and lemongrass in a bowl, and gently mix well.

4 When the fish is ready, remove from the fridge and drain the liquid. Add fish to the chilli sauce mixture, with toasted rice powder and coriander leaves. Mix well and taste – it should be spicy and sour.

5 Divide ceviche among bowls and scatter with coriander leaves.

NOTE You can also use sashimi-grade salmon or tuna for this recipe. Toasted rice powder will keep in an airtight container for up to 1 month.

PREPARE AHEAD Toasted rice powder can be made a day ahead.

WINE MATCH NV Quartz Reef Zero Dosage Méthode Traditionnelle Sparkling, Bendigo.

Prawns with tamarind sauce

SERVES 4 AS A STARTER OR AS PART OF A BANQUET // PREP TIME 40 MINS // COOK 20 MINS

"There is a light, crisp texture created using coconut with rice flour to coat the prawns," says Pen Lee. "Coconut is rich in fibre, good for your health, weight loss and digestion. The tamarind sauce brings a pleasant astringency of sweet and sour."

12	large (660gm) green prawns
	Rice bran oil, for deep-frying
50	gm rice flour
½	tsp baking powder
60	ml coconut cream
80	gm shredded coconut
	Mixed salad greens dressed with lime juice, to serve
	Crisp shallots (optional), thinly sliced spring onion and coriander sprigs, to serve

TAMARIND SAUCE

1½	tbsp olive oil
1	red onion, finely chopped
2	garlic cloves, crushed
125	ml tamarind purée
1½	tbsp soy sauce or tamari, or to taste
40	gm coconut sugar, or to taste
1	tsp cornflour, mixed with 60ml water
	Chilli flakes, to taste

1 For tamarind sauce, heat olive oil in a small saucepan over medium heat. Add onion and garlic, and cook, stirring occasionally, until onion is soft and beginning to turn golden (3-4 minutes). Add tamarind purée, soy sauce and coconut sugar, stirring until sugar dissolves and mixture boils. Add cornflour slurry slowly, stirring until the sauce boils and thickens (1-2 minutes). Stir in chilli flakes to taste and set aside until required.

2 Peel prawns, leaving tails intact, then make a cut down the back of each prawn from the head to the tail end, taking care not to cut all the way through. Remove and discard the vein.

3 Heat oil in a wok over medium heat until 170°C.

4 Meanwhile, sift rice flour, baking powder and a pinch each of salt and pepper into a bowl. Add coconut cream and 1-2 tbsp water to form a thick creamy batter. Holding each prawn by the tail, coat one at a time in the batter, avoiding the tail. Shake gently to remove excess batter, then coat in shredded coconut and place on a tray lined with baking paper.

5 Add prawns to the wok and, in batches, deep-fry until coconut is golden and prawns are just cooked through (2-3 minutes), then drain on paper towel.

6 To serve, divide mixed greens and tamarind sauce among plates and top with prawns. Sprinkle with crisp shallots, if using, spring onion and coriander.

WINE MATCH 2020 Dry River Lovat Gewürztraminer, Martinborough.

ON THE
LAND

Escape to the country at one of these rural retreats surrounded by magnificent gardens or rustic farmland. Discover a historic working sheep farm at Palliser Bay, forage for truffles at Wallingford, stroll manicured English gardens at Tai Tapu and Orinoco Valley, explore lush parklands at Waikato River or tee off for a game of golf at Te Arai.

Wharekauhau

An estate on one of the country's oldest sheep stations at Palliser Bay is a slice of history with a grand Edwardian lodge, luxe cottages, mountain-to-sea vistas, farm-to-table dining and a nearby vineyard.

Located on one of New Zealand's oldest working sheep stations at the foothills of the Remutaka Ranges lies Wharekauhau Country Estate. Just 90 minutes' drive from Wellington, a rural escape awaits at this luxury lodge set on a sprawling estate of ancient forests, rivers and farmland set high above Palliser Bay on the southern tip of the North Island.

At the heart of Wharekauhau stands its grand Edwardian lodge where guests are welcome to relax with a drink by the open fireplace in winter or find a quiet corner in its opulent sitting rooms, library or games room. The lodge also has a heated indoor pool, hot tub, gymnasium, tennis court, petanque field and croquet lawn. Hauora, a Māori philosophy of wellbeing, is the name given to its spa; come here to relax with a mānuka honey facial or green tea warming body wrap and massage.

New Zealand interior designer Virginia Fisher has created a timeless country-chic aesthetic throughout the 16 private cottage suites, all located a short stroll from the main lodge. Each cottage features a king-size bed, heated floors, separate living area, gas fireplace and views of the rugged coastline and Remutaka Ranges. For those seeking the ultimate hideaway villa, the Foley Villa offers complete privacy as well as access to all amenities on the estate. The cottage features three king bedrooms with ensuites and clawfoot baths, separate living and dining areas, a chef's kitchen, wine cellar, study, outdoor fireplace and heated infinity pool. All rooms provide guests with complimentary traditional shortbread – a signature token of country-style hospitality since the lodge first opened.

A farm-to-table ethos is at the centre of Wharekauhau with an emphasis on Wairarapa produce. The open farmhouse kitchen has adopted a locavorian approach, with much of its produce grown and harvested onsite from the orchard, herb and vegetable gardens or foraged from surrounding areas, showcasing the best of the region. The chef sources and forages local produce and ingredients to incorporate into seasonal menus. As a coastal sheep station, lamb is a menu regular, as well as seafood, particularly pāua (abalone) and crayfish from Palliser Bay Farm. Dining is expertly matched with fine vintages from the lodge's well-stocked cellar.

A stay at Wharekauhau isn't complete without a farm tour of its sheep station, magnificent gardens and orchards. Explore the estate's 3000 acres by quad or mountain bike or on foot. Further afield, visit the iconic Cape Palliser Lighthouse and seal colony. A tour of Martinborough, known for its pinot noir and chardonnay, and home to sister vineyards, Te Kairanga and Martinborough Vineyard is a must-visit for wine lovers.

EXPLORE

• Book a wine tour and dinner at Wharekauhau's sister property, Te Kairanga Vineyard, in nearby Martinborough, also owned by US-based wine and sports magnate Bill Foley.

• Take a tour of Wharekauhau's sheep station, one of the country's oldest stations, dating back to the 1840s. It has a history of producing the most sought-after stud rams of the Romney breed, the mainstay of the New Zealand sheep industry.

Ravioli doppi of butterfish mornay, spinach and crisp chorizo

MAKES 12 // PREP TIME 1 HR // COOK 35 MINS (PLUS RESTING)

"This dish is a spin-off of an old classic, using an agnolotti method, to incorporate two elements into one," says executive chef Rob Cullen. "Butterfish is also known as greenbone as it is a vegetarian fish which only feeds on kelp."

1 **chorizo (120gm), very thinly sliced into rounds**
200 **gm baby spinach**

PASTA DOUGH
500 **gm "00" flour**
2 **eggs**
3 **egg yolks**
15 **ml extra-virgin olive oil**
100 **ml milk or water, infused with ¼ tsp saffron threads**

BUTTERFISH MOUSSE
350 **gm skinless butterfish fillets, pin-boned, cut into 2cm small cubes**
2 **egg whites**
Zest and juice of 1 lemon
150 **ml pouring cream, chilled**

TOMATO FONDUE
60 **ml extra-virgin olive oil**
500 **gm cherry tomatoes, halved**
1 **tsp dried oregano**
1 **tsp fresh thyme**
2 **garlic cloves, roasted**

GRUYÈRE SAUCE
60 **gm unsalted butter**
60 **gm plain flour**
300 **ml milk**
1 **tbsp Dijon mustard**
50 **gm grated Gruyère**

1 For pasta dough, place ingredients in a food processor with a pinch of salt and process until a dough forms. Turn out onto a lightly floured surface and knead until smooth and elastic (3-5 minutes), then wrap in plastic wrap and rest at room temperature (20 minutes).

2 Meanwhile, for butterfish mousse, place butterfish, egg whites, lemon zest and juice in a food processor and process to a smooth paste. With the motor running, gradually add chilled cream, processing to just combine. Transfer to a piping bag fitted with a plain nozzle and refrigerate until required.

3 For tomato fondue, place ingredients in a saucepan over a very low heat and cook, stirring occasionally, to infuse and soften tomatoes (20 minutes). Season to taste.

4 For Gruyère sauce, melt butter in a saucepan over medium heat, add flour and stir until sandy-coloured (2-3 minutes). Add milk in batches, whisking until smooth. Bring to the boil, whisking continuously, until mixture boils and thickens. Remove from heat and whisk in mustard and cheese. Season to taste. Transfer Gruyère sauce to a piping bag fitted with a plain nozzle and set aside at room temperature.

5 To roll out pasta, divide dough into four, then, working with one piece at a time, feed through pasta machine rollers, starting at the widest setting. Lightly flour dough as you fold and feed it through, reducing setting notch by notch until pasta is 3mm thick. You will have four 12cm x 50cm pasta sheets.

6 Lay pasta sheets out on a lightly floured surface. Cut each pasta sheet into three 12cm x 16.5cm rectangles. With a long side in front of you, pipe a 5cm long x 2cm strip of mousse, then on the other half of the rectangle pipe a 5cm x 2cm strip of Gruyère sauce (about 1 tbsp of each mixture), leaving 2cm at each end unfilled. Lightly brush the other side with water, then fold the empty half of the pasta strip over the filling and press down to seal. Pinch dough on either side of filling, sealing the dough and creating pillow shapes around the two mounds to remove air pockets. Trim the bottom edge with a crinkle-edged pasta or pastry wheel. Stand the double ravioli up on its base, then bring the two short ends around, brush with water and press to join. Place on a tray and refrigerate, uncovered, to firm or until ready to cook (1-4 hours).

7 In two batches, add ravioli to a large saucepan of boiling salted water and cook until al dente (3-4 minutes). Drain on a tray.

8 Meanwhile, cook chorizo in a frying pan over medium heat, turning frequently until crisp (3-5 minutes), then drain on paper towel. Add spinach to the fat in the pan and cook until wilted (2 minutes).

9 To serve, place a ravioli on each plate with tomato fondue, crisp chorizo and wilted spinach.

WINE MATCH 2006 Mt Difficulty Dry Riesling, Bannockburn.

Smoked lamb shoulder with salsa verde

SERVES 6 // PREP TIME 30 MINS // COOK 4 HRS (PLUS PREHEATING BARBECUE, RESTING)

"This dish represents all that's good about slow cooking," says Cullen. "It is perfect done on the barbecue, and slow cooking the lamb will render the meat tender, juicy and tasty. It's a minimum investment of time and effort for a maximum lamb experience."

1.5	**kg lamb shoulder (see note)**
4	**kg charcoal briquettes**
	Smoking wood chunk, such as wattle, red box or yellow box
	Cider vinegar, to spritz

SPICE RUB

1	**tbsp ground coffee**
1	**tbsp sweet or smoked paprika**
1	**tbsp ground cumin**
1	**tbsp sea salt flakes**
2	**tsp freshly ground black pepper**
60	**ml extra-virgin olive oil**

SALSA VERDE

1	**garlic clove, finely grated on a Microplane**
2	**anchovy fillets**
2	**cups (firmly packed) flat-leaf parsley**
1	**cup (firmly packed) mint**
160	**ml extra-virgin olive oil**
1½	**tbsp red wine vinegar**

1 For spice rub, combine ingredients in a bowl. Place lamb on a tray and rub all over with spice mixture.

2 Meanwhile, to prepare barbecue, place a couple of sheets of newspaper in the bottom of a charcoal chimney starter. Place 12 charcoal briquettes on top of the chimney starter and light the newspaper. Allow the briquettes to burn until they're all completely covered in a thin layer of ash (15-20 minutes).

3 On the bottom rack of a kettle barbecue, place about two-thirds of the bag of unused briquettes into the centre of the barbecue, then build a circle three-quarters of the way around the perimeter of the barbecue, two briquettes wide. Place another two-briquette-wide layer on top and reserve any extra briquettes.

4 Place a 20cm-square disposable roasting pan on the side of the barbecue opposite the briquette chain. Using tongs, carefully place the lit briquettes at one end of the briquette chain so the lit briquettes are just nestled against the unlit ones. Place a chunk of wood where the lit and unlit briquettes meet and place three more chunks of wood on top of the briquette chain at 5cm intervals (this allows them to ignite about every 30-45 minutes). Pour boiling water into the disposable pan.

5 Position the top barbecue grate in place, then close the lid and monitor the temperature inside the barbecue (a digital probe thermometer resting on the top grate is best for this). Open or close the lid vents as needed to maintain a constant 120°C.

6 Place lamb, fat-side up, on the side of the barbecue grate opposite the briquettes and above the water pan. Make sure the fatter end of the lamb is facing towards the lit briquettes. Fold a 30cm-square piece of foil in half and place it under the part of the lamb facing the lit briquettes so it acts as a shield from the fire. Place the lid on the barbecue with the vents directly above the lamb so the smoke carries over the lamb as it exits the barbecue. Maintain the temperature of the barbecue between 110°C and 120°C, adjusting the vent as needed.

7 Smoke lamb, spritzing with cider vinegar every 30 minutes, for 2 hours. Remove lamb from barbecue and wrap in a 60cm x 75cm piece of unwaxed butcher's paper or foil. Return to the barbecue and cover. Cook until meat reaches an internal temperature of 60°C-66°C (2 hours). Rest lamb on a wire rack for 15 minutes before serving.

8 Meanwhile, for salsa verde, place garlic, anchovies and herbs in a food processor and process until finely chopped, Add oil and vinegar, and process until combined. Alternatively, place ingredients into a large mortar and pestle and pound dry ingredients together until smooth, working oil and vinegar until smooth and emulsified. Season to taste. Set aside in the fridge until required. Makes 1 cup.

9 To serve, carve lamb and serve with salsa verde and your favourite sides.

NOTE A 1.5kg lamb will take 4 hours to smoke, 2kg will take 4½ hours and 3kg will need 5½ hours. Ensure the lamb shoulder is removed from the fridge 1 hour before cooking so that the meat reaches room temperature and that the rub will impart more flavour into the meat.

WINE MATCH 2018 Martinborough Vineyard Home Block Pinot Noir, Martinborough.

Otahuna Lodge

As the finest example of Queen Anne architecture in the country, this historic lodge near Christchurch promises luxury suites fit for royalty, elegant farm-to-table dining and Kew-inspired manicured gardens.

Less than 30 minutes from Christchurch, Otahuna Lodge at the foothills of the Banks Peninsula is the finest example of Queen Anne architecture in New Zealand, and scores the highest rating with the New Zealand Historic Places Trust. Built in 1895 by Canterbury pioneer Sir Heaton Rhodes as a wedding present for his wife, the homestead is an enduring gift to those lucky enough to visit.

Every detail at Otahuna Lodge – New Zealand's largest private historic estate – exudes the elegant luxury that defines its grand 19th-century architectural style. The Rhodes Suite offers a palatial master bedroom with ensuite, Victorian fireplace, study and private balcony. The Verandah Suite has a private 14-metre verandah with panoramic views of the Canterbury Plains and Southern Alps. Each of the other five suites retain the homestead's elegant architectural features with ornate fireplaces, carved inglenooks and stained-glass windows. All suites include super-king beds, custom-made linens, deep bathtubs with separate showers, original artworks and bespoke toiletries.

Dining at Otahuna is an epicurean delight with its estate-to-plate philosophy imbued in each of the kitchen's dishes. The daily changing menu celebrates local produce with an emphasis on seasonal estate-grown offerings. The property's vast potager garden and orchards annually supply more than 125 different varieties of organic fruits, mushrooms, nuts and vegetables. Dinner is a four-course chef's dégustation menu that elegantly showcases the estate's seasonal produce. Guests can choose from a range of private locations in which to enjoy the lodge's farm-to-table dining. The wine cellar offers a selection of Canterbury and New Zealand wines to complement each course.

Wander through the lodge's 30 acres of spectacular century-old gardens originally designed by a team from London's Kew Gardens. Wide vistas over lawn and lake contrast beautifully with intimate walks which wind through heavily wooded areas. Some one million daffodils bloom each spring in the Daffodil Paddock. Meanwhile the formal Dutch Garden invites guests to meander its hedged pathways to discover exotic trees, including some of New Zealand's largest and finest specimens.

The lodge's close proximity to Christchurch makes it the ideal place from which to explore Canterbury. Wineries, private gardens, championship golf courses, world-class fishing and even the world's rarest Hector's dolphins are all just a short drive – or helicopter ride – from the lodge's front door.

EXPLORE

• Spend a day exploring the lodge's 30 acres of manicured gardens originally planted by a team from Kew Gardens in the late 1800s.

• Explore North Canterbury wine region to taste some of the country's best vintages. Or set sail in the harbour at Akaroa, home to Hector's dolphins.

Whitebait salad with spring asparagus, pickled lemon and baby herbs

SERVES 6 // PREP TIME 30 MINS // COOK 10 MINS

"What better way to herald spring's arrival than with this fresh, zingy dish filled with the season's delights, including pickled lemon, young asparagus and that oh-so-New Zealand treasured delicacy of just-caught whitebait?" says executive chef Jimmy McIntyre.

2 bunches asparagus (350gm), trimmed
2 tbsp extra-virgin olive oil
40 gm soft butter
600 gm small whitebait (see note)
3 cups mixed micro herbs (basil, rocket, flat-leaf parsley, bull's blood and mizuna)
2 wedges preserved lemon, rind only, cut into thin strips
Avocado oil and lemon juice, for drizzling

1 Place asparagus in a large saucepan of boiling salted water and cook until almost tender but still with some crunch (2 minutes). Drain and refresh in a bowl of iced water, then drain again. Cut each asparagus spear into three on the diagonal, then set aside.

2 Heat a large non-stick frying pan over a high heat. Add half each of the olive oil and butter and swirl pan until butter melts and begins to foam and brown. Working quickly, add half the whitebait and cook, turning, until just cooked through (2 minutes). Season with flaked sea salt and freshly ground pepper. Transfer onto a baking tray. Repeat with remaining olive oil, butter and whitebait.

3 Scatter the asparagus and preserved lemon on top of the mixed micro herbs. Toss salad and whitebait together gently until combined, using tongs or gloved hands.

4 Divide whitebait salad among plates, drizzle with avocado oil and a squeeze of lemon juice.

NOTE If you are unable to get small New Zealand whitebait or if it is a little larger or frozen, toss the whitebait in a thin tempura batter before cooking.

WINE MATCH 2020 Pyramid Valley Sauvignon + Sauvignon Blanc, Pinot Gris, Muscat, North Canterbury.

Quince and hazelnut frangipane tart

SERVES 12 // PREP TIME 1 HR // COOK 7 HRS 15 MINS (PLUS REFRIGERATION, COOLING)

"At Otahuna we reap the many benefits of a century-old orchard, and while we have only four quince trees they produce an astonishing supply of the delicately sweet, juicy fruit," says McIntyre. "Matched with hazelnut and sweet pastry, this dessert is one of autumn's most welcome delights." You will need to poach the quince a day ahead.

3 large quinces (350gm each)
Juice of 1 lemon, squeezed into
600ml water
600 gm caster sugar
900 ml water
1 lemon, quartered
Icing sugar, for dusting
Vanilla-bean ice-cream or
whipped cream, to serve

SWEET TART PASTRY
300 gm plain flour
75 gm icing sugar, sieved
125 gm cold unsalted butter, chopped
1 egg
1-2 tsp ice-cold water

HAZELNUT FRANGIPANE
140 gm unsalted butter, softened
150 gm caster sugar
1 tbsp plain flour
2 eggs, beaten with
½ tsp vanilla extract
150 gm ground hazelnuts

1 For quince, preheat oven to 130°C. Peel the quinces and remove and discard the cores, then cut them into quarters. Add them into the water that has been acidulated with lemon juice (this helps to stop discolouration). Place sugar, water and lemon quarters in an ovenproof pan or flameproof casserole over low heat and cook, stirring, until sugar dissolves. When the syrup boils, add the drained quinces then return to the boil. Cover the surface with a cartouche then cover the pan with a tight-fitting lid and transfer to the oven. Cook until tender and the fruit is a deep crimson colour and soft (6 hours). Remove from the oven and cool the quince in the syrup.

2 For sweet tart pastry, place flour, icing sugar and a pinch of salt in a food processor and pulse. Add butter and pulse until mixture resembles breadcrumbs. Add egg and water and pulse until mixture just comes together as a ball. Transfer dough to a lightly floured surface and pat into a disc. Wrap in baking paper and refrigerate to rest (1 hour).

3 Remove pastry from fridge 10 minutes before rolling out. Grease a 26cm fluted tart tin with removable base. Roll out pastry between two sheets of baking paper until 5mm thick and use it to line prepared tin, leaving a 2cm overhang. Refrigerate to rest (30 minutes).

4 Meanwhile, for hazelnut frangipane, place butter and sugar in a food processor and process until pale and creamy. Add the flour. With the motor running, slowly add egg mixture. Add ground hazelnuts and process until combined.

5 Preheat oven to 190°C. Blind-bake tart until edges are golden (15 minutes), then remove baking weights and paper. Return to the oven, reduce temperature to 180°C and bake until pale golden and dry (10-12 minutes). Set aside to cool or until required.

6 To finish tart, preheat oven to 180°C. Remove quince from cooking syrup and drain on paper towel. Arrange quince quarters (or wedges) to cover the base of the tart shell. Pour over hazelnut frangipane and smooth over quince with an offset spatula. Bake the tart until a skewer inserted in the centre comes out clean and dry (45 minutes). Cover the top of the tart with foil if it is overbrowning.

7 Stand tart for 10 minutes before unmoulding. Dust with icing sugar and cut into 12. Serve with vanilla bean ice-cream or whipped cream.

NOTE This tart can also be made with poached pears or apples and you can also substitute ground almond for the hazelnuts. Leftover syrup can be used in cocktails, with soda over ice, over pancakes, waffles or French toast.

PREPARE AHEAD Quince and pastry can be made a day ahead or the tart can be made a day ahead and warmed.

WINE MATCH 2016 Akarua Vintage Brut, Central Otago.

Huka Lodge

One of New Zealand's oldest and most exclusive luxury lodges offers a secluded retreat in a wooded oasis on the Waikato River with the finest in regional dining and a world of aquatic adventures at nearby Lake Taupō.

Set among lush gardens along the banks of the Waikato River near Lake Taupō on New Zealand's North Island, it's easy to see why Huka Lodge has gained its reputation as a world-class retreat. With humble beginnings nearly a century ago as a fishermen's camp of white canvas tents dotted along the river's edge, today Huka Lodge stands out as one of New Zealand's oldest and celebrated luxury lodges.

The lodge is decorated in interior designer Virginia Fisher's trademark luxurious yet pared-back style. Twenty opulent guest suites are fit for royalty with tranquil river views, king beds with monogrammed linen, palatial bathrooms with heated floors and deep bathtubs. The Alan Pye Cottage and Alex van Heeren Cottage offer next-level seclusion with extra bedrooms, expansive lounge areas, open fireplaces, infinity pools and plunge spas, manicured gardens and outdoor pavilions, perfect for families or friends travelling together.

Dining at Huka Lodge is at the heart of the tradition of generous hospitality for which the lodge is renowned. Showcasing New Zealand's finest, often sustainably produced ingredients and complemented by a magnificent selection of wine, the daily changing menus at Huka Lodge reflect the seasons.

Menu staples include beef and lamb from the North Island, Mahurangi oysters from Auckland and freshly picked fruit and vegetables from regional farmlands. Guests can choose to dine in the main lodge or in one of the many unique dining locations dotted around the grounds, from the wine cellar to the orchard or jetty pavilion.

With a host of unique Taupō experiences at its doorstep, guests can honour the lodge's original fisherman, Irishman Alan Pye, with a spot of trout fly fishing on the banks of the Waikato River. Other aquatic adventures include whitewater rafting, jet boating along the Waikato to the base of Huka Falls or a scenic tour of Lake Taupō on a luxury cruiser taking in views of the mountains, Māori rock carvings and secluded bays. Land adventures include wilderness hiking, playing golf at two world-class courses and a visit to Rotorua's famous geothermal springs. For a meaningful connection, meet a member of the local tribe, Ngāti Tūwharetoa, in an unforgettable Ata Mai Māori Cultural Experience. The lodge offers half or full day helicopter adventures for a breathtaking aerial view of the North Island.

Closer to home, guests can choose from a range of activities including yoga, petanque, croquet and tennis or unwind with a relaxing facial or massage.

EXPLORE

• Go fly fishing for trout in Taupō's rivers just as travellers who came to the area did almost a century ago. Ask the chefs to prepare your catch for lunch or dinner.

• Visit the dramatic Huka Falls located downstream from the lodge, then walk along the Waikato River in the nearby Spa Thermal Park.

Mount Cook Alpine salmon confit with white asparagus, pickled lemon, citrus beurre blanc and salmon roe

SERVES 4 // PREP TIME 30 MINS // COOK 1½ HRS (PLUS OVERNIGHT INFUSING)

"To showcase the clean flavours of the salmon, we poach it very gently in a herb oil and pair it with a citrus sauce to cut through the lovely rich fats from the fish," says executive chef Paul Froggatt. You will need to infuse the oil a day ahead.

4	skinless salmon fillets (150gm each), pin-boned
4	thick white or green asparagus spears, about 1.5cm diameter, trimmed (see note)
200	gm butter, chopped
	Small picked herbs (chervil, dill) and pansy petals, tiny croûtons and chive oil or extra-virgin olive oil, to serve
40	gm salmon roe

HERB OLIVE OIL

1	litre olive oil
2	garlic cloves
2	rosemary sprigs
4	thyme sprigs
2	tsp black peppercorns

CITRUS BEURRE BLANC

125	ml dry white wine
80	ml freshly squeezed orange juice
2	tbsp freshly squeezed grapefruit juice
1	tbsp crème fraîche
200	gm unsalted cold butter, diced
2	tsp lemon juice

PEA PURÉE

250	gm frozen peas, thawed
20	gm butter, chopped
1	golden shallot, finely chopped
40	gm crème fraîche
	Freshly grated nutmeg, to taste

1 For herb olive oil, place olive oil with garlic, herbs and peppercorns in a saucepan over low heat and heat to 70°C with a cooking thermometer. Maintain the oil at this temperature to infuse the flavours for 1 hour, then remove from the heat and stand overnight for flavours to infuse further.

2 To cook salmon, line the base of a large saucepan large enough to fit salmon with baking paper. Strain infused oil into the pan and discard solids. Heat oil to 42°C over low heat with a cooking thermometer. Cook salmon in the oil for 23 minutes, ensuring the salmon is well covered in the oil.

3 Meanwhile, for citrus beurre blanc, place wine in a small saucepan over medium heat and simmer until reduced by three-quarters and the colour of the reduction darkens. Add orange and grapefruit juice and simmer until reduced to 60ml (5 minutes). Add crème fraîche, bring to the simmer, then reduce heat to very low and add butter a little at a time, whisking continuously, until incorporated. Season to taste with salt and lemon juice. Keep warm until needed but do not allow to get too hot or the emulsion will separate.

4 For pea purée, place peas in a saucepan of boiling salted water and cook until tender. Drain, refresh in iced water, then drain again on paper towel. Heat butter in a small saucepan over low-medium heat, add shallots and stir until softened (3 minutes). Add peas and mix well to coat in butter mixture. Add crème fraîche and blend with a stick blender to a smooth purée. Season with salt and fresh nutmeg. Keep warm or transfer to a container and refrigerate until required.

5 For white asparagus, peel the ends. Melt butter in a small frying pan over medium heat, add asparagus and cook, turning, until tender and butter is nut brown (6 minutes).

6 To serve, place an asparagus spear on each plate and garnish the length with small picked herbs (chervil and dill) and pansy petals. Drain salmon fillets on paper towel and place on plates. Place a spoonful of pea purée beside and using the back of a spoon, make an indent in the centre. Arrange chervil leaves around the edge with tiny croûtons and fill the indent with a little chive or olive oil. Stir the salmon roe into the beurre blanc and serve on the side.

NOTE If white asparagus is unavailable, substitute thick blanched green asparagus and omit the brown butter.

PREPARE AHEAD Herb olive oil can be made a day ahead.

WINE MATCH 2019 Mount Edward Pinot Blanc, Central Otago.

Kombu-cured tuna with green apple, lemon verbena cream and buttermilk dressing

SERVES 8 // PREP TIME 45 MINS (PLUS INFUSING)

"This dish was created to replicate the scales on top of the fish," says Froggatt. **"The lemon verbena and buttermilk in the dressing brings a pleasant acidity and creaminess to the dish."**

600 gm piece tuna (albacore or yellowfin)
1 Granny Smith apple, peeled
1 kohlrabi, peeled
Segmented lime pieces and
nasturtium leaves, to serve

CURE
2 tsp juniper berries
1 tsp white peppercorns
30 gm ginger, coarsely chopped
2 garlic cloves, coarsely chopped
750 gm rock salt
75 gm caster sugar
Finely grated zest of 1 lime
2 large kombu sheets (18cm x 22cm)

LEMON VERBENA OIL
250 gm fruit-style extra-virgin olive oil
1 cup (lightly packed) lemon
verbena leaves (see note)

LEMON VERBENA CREAM
100 gm lemon juice
25 gm caster sugar
50 gm Isomalt powder (see note)
½ tsp ascorbic powder (see note)
1.5 titanium-strength gelatine leaves
Chlorophyll (see note)

BUTTERMILK DRESSING
250 gm buttermilk
125 gm Kewpie mayonnaise
Lemon verbena oil (recipe above)

1 For cure, place juniper berries, peppercorns, ginger and garlic in a food processor and process until finely crushed. Add rock salt, sugar and lime zest and process until well combined. Rinse 1 sheet of kombu until softened then place in a 22cm x 25cm glass or plastic dish. Place half the salt mixture on top then nestle tuna in salt. Cover with remaining salt and spice cure. Soften the second sheet of kombu and place over the cure-covered tuna. Refrigerate until cured (1 hour). Once cured, brush off the salt mix and leave to rest in the fridge for 1-2 hours to help the cure penetrate the tuna.
2 For lemon verbena oil, place ingredients in a high-speed blender and blend until very smooth (2 minutes). Transfer to a jug and stand to infuse (8 hours or overnight). Strain through a fine sieve and set aside until required.
3 For lemon verbena cream, place lemon juice, sugar, Isomalt powder and ascorbic powder in a small saucepan over medium heat. Bring to the boil, stirring to dissolve sugar. Meanwhile, soften gelatine in a bowl of cold water (3-5 minutes) then add to the pan and stir to dissolve. Transfer to a blender and blend on high speed (1 minute) then gradually add 200ml of the lemon verbena oil and check the seasoning. Leave to set and then whisk just before serving to make a smooth cream. Add ½ tsp chlorophyll to remaining lemon verbena oil to tint bright green.
4 For buttermilk dressing, whisk ingredients together in a bowl and season to taste.
5 For apple and kohlrabi rounds, cut apple and kohlrabi into 3mm-thick slices with a mandolin, then cut into rounds with a 2cm cutter. Toss apple with 2 tsp green lemon verbena oil.
6 To serve, cut the tuna into 1cm dice. Place an 8cm ring mould in a shallow bowl and fill with tuna, then add a few dots of the lemon verbena cream on top. Carefully lift off the mould and layer the apple and kohlrabi rounds to make a fish-scale-like pattern. Add a few more dots of the lemon verbena cream around the tuna and pour buttermilk dressing on the side, add a few drops of green lemon verbena oil and swirl into the dressing. Garnish with lime segment pieces and nasturtium leaves. Repeat with remaining ingredients.

NOTE Lemon verbena is available from nurseries and specialist greengrocers. Isomalt powder is made from sugar beets and is a type of sugar alcohol. It is used in this recipe for its holding capacities. You can use vitamin C powder, available from pharmacies, instead of ascorbic powder to help retain the fresh green colour of the lemon verbena cream. To make chlorophyll, blanch green spinach, refresh, then finely chop. Squeeze in muslin for a concentrated green colouring.

PREPARE AHEAD Lemon verbena oil and buttermilk dressing can be made a day ahead.

WINE MATCH 2021 Te Whare Ra Toru Gewürztraminer, Riesling and Pinot Gris, Marlborough.

Edenhouse

Although no longer open to guests, we pay homage to the hospitality legacy of this traditional English country-style lodge in the Orinoco Valley with its picturesque designer gardens and regional seasonal fare.

Nestled in a picturesque pocket of the Orinoco Valley in the foothills of the Kahurangi National Park, Edenhouse is a secret-garden hideaway that has set the benchmark for personalised hospitality for nearly 16 years. While the custodianship of this inviting home away from home has, in 2022, been transferred to a private family estate, in the spirit of sharing New Zealand's finest experiences, we share a little piece of its hospitality legacy through the recipes included in this book.

After years of living abroad, Peter and Bobbie Martin returned to Bobbie's New Zealand homeland in 2002 and began the transformation of 50 acres of farmland from blank canvas to a garden lover's paradise that lives up to the property's name. They designed the elegant country residence within its 16-acre gardens drawing on Bobbie's design skills honed at Inchbald School of Design and The English Gardening School at the famous Chelsea Physic Garden.

The Martins opened their doors to welcome guests to their charming English country-style residence in 2006. In the years since opening Edenhouse, their exclusive hideaway, impeccable taste, regionally inspired dining experience and genuinely warm welcome earned Edenhouse an impressive clutch of international accolades and a loyal following of guests from around the world that returned to this idyllic haven year after year.

Shared dining experiences were always a highlight of any stay. The Martins' Edenhouse menu always drew inspiration and ingredients from their abundant gardens, talented neighbours, the nearby rivers and surrounding fertile farmlands. Visitors to the region can continue to enjoy a rich bounty of regional fare at the many local cellar doors and craft breweries, at farm gates and farmers' markets, in award-winning restaurants and from trout-filled rivers. The Nelson Tasman region is renowned for its stone fruits but also produces some of the world's best apples and berries, handcrafted wines and craft beers, cheeses, truffles, olive oils and ciders.

Venture only moments further afield, and the Abel Tasman National Park, its pristine bushlands fringed by golden beaches, invites outdoor adventures from hiking and kayaking to canyoning, swimming and sailing. Cycling trails weave through orchards and vineyards, alongside rivers and on forest trails to connect vibrant local villages and thriving arts and crafts communities. Fishing enthusiasts will also appreciate the nearby Motueka and Karamea Rivers which offer some of the country's best trout fishing adventures.

EXPLORE

• Hike through spectacular Mount Arthur in Kahurangi National Park, just a 15-minute drive from Edenhouse.

• Visit the small village of Upper Moutere, home to local artisans, winemakers, cheesemakers, ceramic artists, sculptors and producers.

Fillet of beef with white truffle butter, steamed vegetables and salad of miner's lettuce

SERVES 6 // PREP TIME 15 MINS // COOK 3 HRS 40 MINS (PLUS STANDING, RESTING)

"This recipe uses South Island fillet of beef and local truffles grown by Neudorf Mushrooms who have been supplying mushrooms for more than 20 years," says chef Sarah Parkes. "They also grow saffron milk cap mushrooms and other specialist produce."

1.4 kg fillet of beef
1 tsp wild mushroom and herb salt (see note)
1 tbsp finely chopped rosemary
1 tbsp freshly ground black pepper
2 tbsp olive oil
30 gm butter
Steamed broccoli and asparagus tossed in lemon-infused extra-virgin olive oil and salad of miner's lettuce (see note), to serve

TRUFFLE BUTTER
200 gm unsalted butter, softened
10 gm white truffle, grated on a Microplane (see note)
½ tsp fine sea salt
2 tsp walnut oil
⅛ tsp freshly ground black pepper

1 For beef, trim and tie fillet of beef with kitchen string at 4cm intervals to form an even shape. Place beef in a large roasting pan and rub with mushroom salt, chopped rosemary and pepper and bring to room temperature (1 hour).

2 Preheat oven to 75°C. Drizzle beef with half the oil then roast until meat reaches an internal temperature of 55°C-60°C on a meat thermometer for medium-rare (3½ hours).

3 Meanwhile, for truffle butter, mix ingredients together in a bowl until combined. Place butter mixture on a piece of baking paper and form into a log, wrap in baking paper, then twist ends like a bon-bon to compact the butter log. Refrigerate until required.

4 Heat remaining oil in a large frying pan or flameproof roasting pan over high heat. Add beef and cook, turning, for 5 minutes or until browned all over. Transfer beef to a tray. Rest, loosely covered with foil, for 15 minutes.

5 To serve, remove string from beef and cut into thick slices. Serve with a slice of truffle butter and steamed vegetables tossed in lemon oil and a salad of miner's lettuce.

NOTE There are many types of wild mushroom salts available, choose whichever you can get your hands on. Miner's lettuce is a rounded succulent-type plant with a small edible white flower. The high vitamin C content made it popular with miners during the gold rush, hence the name. Substitute green mustard cress and watercress leaves. Fresh white truffles (borchii) are seasonal and available from late autumn to early spring. If unavailable, substitute black truffles.

PREPARE AHEAD Truffle butter can be made a day ahead.

WINE MATCH 2018 Man O' War Ironclad Bordeaux Blend, Waiheke Island.

Tarte Tatin

SERVES 6 // PREP TIME 50 MINS // COOK 40 MINS (PLUS RESTING)

"Use sweet, fragrant heritage apples for the best flavour," recommends Parkes. "Tarte Tatin in my experience is a real winner to conclude an autumn or winter meal."

Double cream, to serve

PASTRY
170 gm plain flour
55 gm ground rice
140 gm butter, chopped
55 gm caster sugar
1 egg, beaten

TOPPING
110 gm butter
110 gm granulated sugar
7 Granny Smith apples
Grated zest of 1 lemon

1 Preheat oven to 190°C.

2 To make pastry, sift flour and ground rice into a large bowl. Rub in the butter until the mixture resembles breadcrumbs. Stir in caster sugar, then add the egg and bring the dough together. Turn out onto a bench, shape into a disc, then wrap in plastic wrap and refrigerate to rest and firm (1 hour).

3 To make topping, melt butter in a 25cm cast-iron or heavy-based stainless-steel frying pan with a metal handle. Add granulated sugar and remove from heat. Peel the apples and remove the cores then cut into quarters. Arrange apple quarters over the melted butter and sugar in the base of the frying pan then sprinkle with grated lemon zest.

4 Place the frying pan over high heat until the butter and sugar start to caramelise (6-7 minutes). It is essential that the apples get dark. Remove from the heat.

5 Roll pastry out on a lightly floured bench into a 32cm round, 5mm-thick, to fit the top of the pan. (This pastry will be short.) Lay pastry over apples and press down lightly, tucking the pastry edge into the side of the pan with a spoon. Using a small sharp knife, score the pastry two or three times to allow the steam to escape. Transfer to oven and bake until pastry is dark golden (25-30 minutes).

6 Remove from oven and stand for 5 minutes. Place a plate on top and shake to loosen tart. Working quickly and very carefully (the caramel will be hot), invert tart onto the plate. Cut into pieces and serve hot with cream.

PREPARE AHEAD Pastry can be made a day ahead.

WINE MATCH 2021 Framingham F-Series Auslese Riesling, Marlborough.

Te Arai Lodge

A stay at this family-run boutique lodge near Auckland promises a luxury retreat with forest-to-ocean vistas, garden-to-table dining, world-class golf courses and genuine hospitality.

Surrounded by more than 20 acres of ancient podocarp forest and native bush, Te Arai Lodge is set on an elevated ridge with panoramic views of rural landscape, Te Arai beaches and islands off the Mangawhai Coast. Te Arai's breathtaking cliff walks, towering native forests, impressive golf courses and surfers' paradise coastline offer a slice of pure New Zealand.

Owned and operated by Vince and Kathy Moores, Te Arai offers guests the kind of personalised hospitality that only comes from a family-run affair. Daughter Nicola, a talented garden-to-table chef and multilingual host, manages the lodge and heads the kitchen while son Doug, a qualified yoga instructor, keen golfer and artist, teaches organic movement classes at the lodge and is in charge of marketing, reservations, guest activities and new initiatives.

The 750-square-metre lodge accommodates up to 10 guests in four luxury suites and a bunk room and can be booked for exclusive use. The self-contained suites feature superb views, private outdoor bath, organic linen robes, sustainable bathroom products and a complimentary mini bar with activated nuts and freshly baked cookies.

A focal point of the lodge is the Great Room, an atrium-style lounge, dining and kitchen area framed by giant scissor trusses to highlight its soaring ceilings. True to its name, everything is on a grand scale, with its double-sided, stone-clad fireplace and a bespoke kitchen that leads to raised garden beds where freshly grown produce is harvested for the table. Artifacts from the Moores' travels along with local artworks create an intimate, personalised home-like setting.

The lodge's garden-to-table culinary offering reflects the organic produce grown on the estate complemented with local produce including free-range chicken, grass-fed beef and line-caught fish from Leigh. The chef's kitchen gives guests the opportunity to cook their own meals using local organic produce or use one of the lodge's catering services.

A range of outdoor activities to suit all tastes is available at your doorstep. Destined to be a mecca for golf fans, Te Arai Links golf courses, only minutes from the lodge, will feature two premier links golf courses designed by Tom Doak and Coore and Crenshaw Design. Discover why New Zealand is renowned for its spectacular walking trails with a choice of tracks including the Mangawhai Cliff Walk, the Te Arai Sand Dune Walk, the Langs to Waipu Coastal Walk and the Tanekaha Walks that traverse multiple waterfalls, historic kauri dams and native forest. Closer to home, there's no shortage of facilities to keep guests entertained and pampered with a heated saltwater pool, hot tub, sauna, yoga studio, gym and day spa.

EXPLORE

• Hike the Mangawhai Cliff Walk north of Te Arai, one of New Zealand's top 10 walks with spectacular views along the coastline as well as secluded beaches for swimming.

• Browse the Matakana Village Farmers' Market with its incredible produce, food stalls, live music and boutique shops.

Chicken Marbella with roasted kūmara and char-grilled Brussels sprouts

SERVES 6 // PREP TIME 1 HR // COOK 1 HR 40 MINS (PLUS MARINATING)

"To enjoy the bounty of our organic garden all year, we cure and press our own olives, dehydrate our plums, turn pomegranate arils into molasses and pick fresh herbs daily to enhance dishes such as this chicken Marbella," says lodge manager Nicola Moores.

100	gm Sicilian green olives, pitted
100	gm pitted prunes, or dates or dried apricots, halved
50	gm baby capers
6	garlic cloves, crushed
½	cup (firmly packed) oregano leaves
3	bay leaves
60	ml extra-virgin olive oil
60	ml red wine vinegar
1.9	kg organic free-range chicken, cut into 6 pieces
125	ml homemade chicken stock
125	ml dry white wine
60	ml pomegranate molasses
6	kūmara (300gm each) (see note)
60	ml extra-virgin olive oil, plus extra for thinning

MACADAMIA BUTTER

225	gm macadamias
¼	tsp sea salt flakes

CHAR-GRILLED BRUSSELS SPROUTS

600	gm Brussels sprouts, trimmed
80	ml extra-virgin olive oil
3	garlic cloves, thinly sliced
¼	tsp chilli flakes
	Zest and juice of ½ lemon
25	gm parmesan, finely grated

1 Combine olives, prunes, capers, garlic, oregano, bay, oil and vinegar in a large bowl. Season well with sea salt flakes and freshly ground black pepper. Add chicken pieces, toss well to coat, then cover and refrigerate to marinate (2-24 hours).

2 For macadamia butter, preheat oven to 180°C. Place macadamias on a small oven tray and roast, stirring occasionally, until dark golden (5-10 minutes). Reserve 50gm macadamias and roughly chop once cool. Place remaining hot macadamias and salt in a high-speed blender and blend, scraping down the sides of the blender every so often, until a smooth butter forms. Set aside until required.

3 Arrange chicken in a single layer in a roasting pan and spoon over the marinade. Whisk stock, wine and pomegranate molasses together in a jug, then pour over and around the chicken. Bake, basting every so often and turning chicken pieces over halfway through the cooking time, until golden and cooked through (50 minutes-1 hour). The chicken is cooked when the thickest part of the thigh pieces yield clear (not pink) juices when pricked with a carving fork. Set aside to rest for 10 minutes.

4 Meanwhile, peel kūmara and cut each one into six wedges. Transfer to two large oven trays, drizzle with olive oil, season to taste and toss to coat. Add kūmara to oven during last 10 minutes of chicken cooking time. Once chicken has been removed, increase oven to 220°C and roast kūmara for a further 10-15 minutes or until golden.

5 For char-grilled Brussels sprouts, preheat a barbecue on medium-high and bring a large saucepan of water to the boil. Thinly slice 200gm sprouts on a mandolin and soak in a bowl of iced water until required. Blanch remaining sprouts in boiling water until tender crisp (1-2 minutes) then drain and refresh. Drain again, pat dry and cut in half lengthways. Transfer to a large tray, drizzle with 1 tbsp oil, season to taste and toss to coat. Barbecue sprouts until grill marks appear, turning halfway through cooking time (5-10 minutes). Meanwhile, heat remaining oil in a small frying pan over low-medium heat. Add garlic and chilli flakes, and stir until lightly golden (1-2 minutes). Drain sliced Brussels sprouts, transfer to a bowl and toss with 1 tbsp lemon juice.

6 To serve sprouts, spread sliced sprouts on a platter and layer char-grilled sprouts on top. Drizzle over garlic-and-chilli-infused oil. Scatter with parmesan and lemon zest.

7 To serve kūmara, spread two-thirds of the macadamia butter over a platter and layer kūmara on top. Thin remaining macadamia butter with a little extra oil and drizzle over the top. Sprinkle with reserved chopped macadamias.

8 Serve chicken with cooking liquid spooned over. Serve with roasted kūmara with macadamia butter and char-grilled Brussels sprouts.

NOTE We use purple-skin and white-flesh kūmara which goes crisp, orange-skin and flesh kūmara, and when available, the rarer purple-flesh kūmara. We suggest you accompany this dish with a starchy side to soak up all the delicious juices – like cinnamon-spiced couscous. To turn the marinade into more of a sauce, simmer it in a small saucepan until reduced slightly.

WINE MATCH 2017 Mahi Twin Valleys Chardonnay, Marlborough.

Lemon olive oil rosemary cake

SERVES 10 // PREP TIME 20 MINS // COOK 30 MINS

"This fragrant cake embodies garden-to-table food that lies at the very heart of Te Arai Lodge," says Moores. "The seasonal offering of our organic garden is the inspiration for the cake's unique flavour profile that beautifully marries zingy citrus with aromatic rosemary, extra-virgin olive oil and floral mānuka honey. It's deliciously moist with lingering notes of lemon-pine and a lovely textural bite from the sweet toasted almonds."

Buffalo milk yoghurt, blackberries, lemon zest and rosemary sprig, to serve

CAKE
- 100 gm natural almonds, roasted
- 1 piece gluten-free bread (50gm), lightly toasted and coarsely chopped
- 2 tbsp rosemary, coarsely chopped
- 100 gm coconut sugar
- 2 tsp baking powder, sifted
- Zest of 1 lemon
- 4 eggs, lightly beaten
- 150 ml extra-virgin olive oil
- 125 ml lemon juice

LEMON HONEY ROSEMARY SYRUP
- 50 gm mānuka honey
- 2 rosemary sprigs
- 125 ml water
- 160 ml lemon juice

1 For the cake, grease and line the base and sides of a 20cm round springform cake tin with baking paper. Place almonds, bread and rosemary in a food processor, and process until the mixture resembles fine breadcrumbs. Transfer to a bowl, add sugar, baking powder and lemon zest, and mix together. Add eggs, oil and lemon juice, and whisk to combine. Transfer to the tin, place cake inside a cold oven and set the oven to 180°C. Bake until a skewer inserted into the centre of the cake comes out clean (25-30 minutes). Place cake on a wire rack, then set aside to cool in the tin.

2 Meanwhile, for lemon honey rosemary syrup, place ingredients in a small saucepan over medium-high heat. Bring to the boil and stir to combine. Reduce heat to medium and simmer until reduced and thickened slightly (10 minutes). Using a wooden skewer, pierce the top of the cake in several places and drizzle over the hot syrup.

3 Cut the cake into 10 even slices and serve with buffalo milk yoghurt, blackberries and a sprinkling of lemon zest and rosemary sprig.

NOTE If you are not on a gluten-free diet any style of bread can be used in this recipe.

PREPARE AHEAD Cake can be made a day ahead, bring to room temperature before serving.

WINE MATCH NV Kumeu River Crémant, Kumeu.

Wallingford

A historic homestead on a sheep and cattle farm promises an idyllic rural escape with farm-to-plate dining, relaxed hospitality and a natural wonderland perfect for truffle hunting.

From the moment you arrive at the historic Wallingford homestead in Central Hawke's Bay, you'll discover a world that nurtures with slow food, bespoke hospitality and sprawling farmland. Nestled in 2200 acres of a working sheep and cattle station, Wallingford offers an idyllic country retreat for those looking to escape the harried pace of the big smoke.

Built by local MP Jack Ormond in 1853, the Hawke's Bay's largest single-storey homestead was named after his English home town. Wallingford's architecture speaks to the grandeur of yesteryear with open fireplaces to sit by, wide verandahs to take in the verdant vistas, a grand piano for entertainment and a well-stocked library to read in. A private heated pool with its own pavilion overlooks the property's 1800 oak trees grown to cultivate Périgord truffles.

Five of the homestead's nine spacious suites feature ensuites while all come with central heating. Guests are invited to enjoy a complimentary selection of biscuits, cakes and fruit in the reception lounge. For those wanting the house all to themselves, there's a whole house exclusive-use package. The homestead sleeps up to 18 and guests can request a tailored accommodation package with an alfresco dining experience, live jazz or a chef's dégustation prepared tableside in the open-air pool pavilion.

Run by restaurateur Jeanette Woerner with her husband chef Chris Stockdale, Wallingford offers communal dining with a focus on seasonal and foraged produce sourced from local Hawke's Bay producers including Bostock chickens from Hastings, Better Fishing from Ahuriri and fruit and vegetables from Breige in Waipawa. While the estate's herbs, vegetables and Angus beef appear on the menu, the star of the show is its Périgord truffles. The ever-changing eight-course dégustation menu includes the likes of local gurnard, milk and Périgord truffle; 90-day Wallingford dry-aged black Angus with celeriac, chard, beets and peas; snapper, avocado, makrut lime and taewa. Located close to Pōrangahau, the menu is seafood-driven with local fishermen supplying the fresh catch. Wine pairings from a comprehensive list are available for each course.

Guests can join in the many activities at the homestead including hands-on cooking classes, truffle foraging weekends and visits by local winemakers. For creative souls, there's artistic workshops with local artists and a writer's retreat. For those who wish to wander further afield, wineries abound as do bike tracks and local beaches with Pōrangahau the closest. And if you want to explore the art deco capital of New Zealand, Napier is a little more than an hour's drive from the property.

EXPLORE

• Book a winter Truffle Weekend to forage, sample and cook the Périgord truffle from Wallingford's impressive truffle grove of 1800 evergreen oaks.

• Take a farm tour of Wallingford's neighbouring 845-hectare Angus Stud Station for a taste of rural life with its grazing cows and sheep.

'Ice and Fire' trevally, pickled fennel and ginger with radish

SERVES 4 // PREP TIME 20 MINS // COOK 25 MINS (PLUS COOLING)

"Local, low in mercury and gifted with a fast reproductive rate, trevally is the unsung hero," says chef Chris Stockdale. "Its friends on the plate, too, are all locals; sorrel and greens gathered from our garden, and ginger sourced from an organic grower in Waipawa."

100 gm water
100 gm table salt
200 gm ice cubes
200 gm sashimi-quality trevally fillet loin-cut, cleaned of bloodline
6 radishes, thinly sliced
Micro mustard cress, bull's blood and julienne of radicchio, to serve

PICKLED FENNEL AND GINGER
350 gm fennel bulb, trimmed, coarsely chopped (125gm trimmed)
80 gm ginger, coarsely chopped
2 golden shallots, coarsely chopped
125 ml grapeseed oil
100 gm caster sugar
200 ml boiling water
10 gm dashi stock powder
50 ml light soy sauce
400 ml rice wine vinegar
60 ml lime juice
60 ml fish sauce
2 pinches of chilli flakes
100 gm pickled ginger, finely chopped

1 For fish, place water and salt in a small saucepan over medium heat and stir until salt dissolves (3-5 minutes). Transfer to a shallow container, cool then add the ice cubes. Add the fish and leave for 1-2 minutes to firm. (The salt water will reduce the freezing point of the ice and season the fish).

2 Remove fish from iced water, pat dry with paper towel and place on a wire rack placed over an oven tray. While still chilled, sear the fish all over with a kitchen blowtorch until a touch of colour is created (1 minute), turn over and repeat on the other side.

3 For pickled fennel and ginger, place fennel, ginger, shallots and grapeseed oil in a blender and pulse until finely chopped. Transfer ginger mixture to a frying pan over low-medium heat. Cook, stirring frequently, until very soft but without colour (10 minutes). Add sugar, water, dashi stock powder, soy sauce and vinegar. Stir until sugar dissolves then simmer until mixture is reduced by half (20 minutes). Remove from heat, cool, then stir in lime juice, fish sauce, chilli flakes and pickled ginger. Makes 2¼ cups.

4 Using a sharp knife, cut the fish on an angle into 2mm-thick slices. Arrange slices on plates, leaving gaps, then spoon the dressing into the gaps. Garnish with radish, micro mustard cress, bull's blood and radicchio.

NOTE The recipe makes more pickled fennel and ginger than you need, however, it will keep refrigerated for 1 week. Use leftovers on salads, especially, crisp greens and beetroot.

PREPARE AHEAD Pickled fennel and ginger can be made a day ahead.

WINE MATCH 2021 Craggy Range Gimblett Gravels Vineyard Rosé, Hawke's Bay.

Makrut lime, lemon and lime bavarois

SERVES 6 // PREP TIME 45 MINS // COOK 30 MINS (PLUS SETTING, CHILLING, FREEZING)

"Many moons ago, a kind-hearted, culinary soul dedicated a nook of the Wallingford grounds to the growth of all things citrus – yuzu, makrut, mandarins, lemons, limes and cumquats," says Stockdale. "This sweet offering is an adventure seeking to acknowledge both our benefactors and the generosity of the earth."

LEMON CURD

4	egg yolks
175	gm caster sugar
	Zest of 2 lemons
100	ml lemon juice
60	gm unsalted butter, chopped

LIME BAVAROIS

125	ml milk
3	makrut lime leaves, coarsely chopped
90	gm caster sugar
	Zest and juice of 1 lime
4	egg yolks
2	titanium-strength gelatine leaves, softened in cold water (3-5 minutes)
250	ml pouring cream

LIME GRANITA

200	ml water
100	gm caster sugar
200	ml lime juice

BISCUIT

180	gm gluten-free plain flour
1	tsp xanthan gum
½	tsp baking powder
¼	tsp bicarbonate of soda
	Pinch of salt
100	gm caster sugar
100	gm unsalted butter, softened
1	egg, beaten
1	tsp vanilla bean paste
1½	tbsp milk

1 For lemon curd, whisk yolks and sugar in a heatproof bowl to combine, then whisk in lemon zest and juice. Place over a saucepan of simmering water and stir continuously until mixture thickens enough to coat the back of a spoon (7-8 minutes). Whisk in butter until melted and combined. Transfer to a jar and refrigerate until set (2 hours). Lemon curd will keep refrigerated for a week. Makes 280gm.

2 For lime bavarois, place milk and lime leaves in a saucepan over low heat and bring almost to the boil. Meanwhile, whisk sugar, lime zest and juice with egg yolks in a bowl until sugar dissolves. Gradually whisk in hot milk mixture until combined. Return the mixture to the saucepan over low-medium heat and stir until mixture thickens enough to coat the back of a spoon. (Do not allow mixture to boil.) Remove from heat. Squeeze excess water from gelatine, add to custard and stir until dissolved (1 minute). Strain through a fine sieve into a jug, then refrigerate, stirring occasionally until chilled (20 minutes). Whisk cream until soft peaks form, then gently fold whipped cream into custard mixture until just combined. Spoon into six 150ml moulds filling 1cm from the top. Spoon lemon curd into a piping bag fitted with an 8mm nozzle, pipe the lemon curd into the centre of the bavarois until the mixture is 2mm from the top. Place in the fridge to set (4 hours or overnight).

3 For lime granita, place water and sugar in a small saucepan over medium heat and stir until sugar dissolves. Bring to the boil and boil for 1 minute. Remove from heat and cool, then stir in lime juice. Transfer lime syrup to a 20cm x 30cm shallow metal tray and freeze, stirring and scraping occasionally with a fork until crystals start to form and granita is frozen (4-5 hours).

4 For biscuit, preheat oven to 170°C. Place flour, xanthan gum, baking powder, bicarbonate of soda and a pinch of salt into the bowl of a food processor and pulse to combine. Add, sugar, butter, egg and vanilla, and pulse until well combined. Add the milk, and pulse until dough clumps. Using a rolling pin, spread out dough between two sheets of baking paper until 2mm thick. Lift biscuit, still between baking paper, onto an oven tray. Bake with top layer of baking paper covering until golden brown (15 minutes or until the top layer of paper peels away easily). Remove from tray and cool. Store in an airtight container until required. To use, break into random shapes.

5 To serve, invert a bavarois onto a chilled plate, top with biscuit, broken into random shapes, then spoon granita on the side.

PREPARE AHEAD All the elements for this recipe can be prepared a day ahead.

WINE MATCH 2018 De La Terre Late Harvest Viognier, Hawke's Bay.

SARAH FARAG

Owner and director, Southern Crossings New Zealand

Tracing her ancestral ties as far back as New Zealand's first natural tourist attraction of the Pink and White Terraces, together with a lifetime of family travel that instilled immense national pride in her country, it was perhaps inevitable Sarah Farag would forge a career specialising in New Zealand luxury travel. While Sarah's international travel has given her a great appreciation for different cultures and cuisines, it ultimately fuelled her desire to showcase the best of her country's vast treasures and delicious hidden gems to travellers. Sarah now shares this passion with her dedicated team of travel designers at Southern Crossings New Zealand. Based in Auckland and constantly travelling across New Zealand, she now explores the country with her own children. Her little black book is filled with talented local chefs, winemakers, passionate adventurers and guides who can open doors to deliciously unique and authentic experiences, with her favourite foodie finds flavouring the personalised luxury trips from which lifelong memories are made. Sarah's expertise in New Zealand luxury travel and local connections have earned her a place on such coveted international travel lists as *Condé Nast Traveler*'s list of the world's leading travel specialists, *Town & Country*'s list of travel gurus, Wendy Perrin's WOW List and Travel + Leisure's A-List. Spend any time with her, and her passion for travel, pride in her country and ability to connect people are immediately clear — and are echoed by her talented and experienced Southern Crossings team that now celebrates more than 35 years in leading New Zealand travel experiences.

southern-crossings.com

Acknowledgements

New Zealand's fine wine and fabulous food have attracted, and delighted, visitors from around the globe for decades. As Southern Crossings celebrates 35 years of sharing New Zealand's finest travel experiences with the most discerning travellers from around the globe, it seemed most fitting to share a collection of our favourite travel experiences that flavour our carefully tailored journeys across the country.

New Zealand's truly world-class food and wine experiences are created with the finest local produce, curated by a collection of talented artisans, winemakers and chefs, and enjoyed in some of the most spectacular settings.

In recognition of how New Zealand's culinary experience has evolved over the years and its integral role in flavouring our guests' travel experiences, it was our intention with this book to share some of New Zealand's most amazing travel experiences through the epicurean experiences they offer.

My heartfelt thanks to the many people and partners who have brought this project to life, including all of the people associated with the very special properties featured in these pages who not only inspired this book, but so generously opened their kitchens and shared their stories, and whose support helped make this book possible. Grateful thanks to Auckland Unlimited and Hawke's Bay Tourism, for their support of the exceptional food and wine experiences that their regions give rise to.

A big thank you to the *Gourmet Traveller* team who have so beautifully brought our vision to life.

An enormous thanks to my fellow Southern Crossings directors and the entire Southern Crossings team, including the travel designers who passionately curate and share New Zealand's most rewarding travel experiences with a dedication that only comes from a genuine love of what they do, and for which I am very grateful every day.

And thank you to our collaborators, Bettina Kramer and Sara Devenie, whose support and loyalty, ensured this project came to fruition.

Finally, thank you to you, the reader, the foodie, the discerning traveller – we hope you enjoy this book as much as we have enjoyed creating it.

Sarah Farag

TĀMAKI MAKAURAU AUCKLAND

Tāmaki Makaurau Auckland is an urban oasis. It's where sparkling waters and lush landscapes meet city sophistication. World-class shopping and phenomenal dining are never too far from harbours, islands, native bush and black-sand beaches. Go sky diving or whale watching, hike an ancient volcanic cone, sip local award-winning wine, or star gaze from the International Dark Sky Sanctuary of Great Barrier Island.

A multicultural city bursting with life, Tāmaki Makaurau Auckland offers a host of rich cultural, creative and sporting events, festivals and theatre productions.

Don't miss the chance to experience New Zealand's unique Māori culture and come to know our manaakitanga – hospitality, generosity and openness of spirit – as you connect with our people, land and the stories that have shaped our place. Auckland was recently named the number one city to visit in *Lonely Planet's Best in Travel 2022*.

AUCKLAND UNLIMITED is the region's economic and cultural agency responsible for delivering co-ordinated, region-wide programmes to maximise cultural, social and economic benefits for residents and visitors. *aucklandunlimited.com*

HAWKE'S BAY TOURISM

Hawke's Bay Tourism is the Regional Tourism Organisation for Hawke's Bay, New Zealand's food and wine country. Encompassing Central Hawke's Bay, Hastings and Wairoa districts and Napier city, Hawke's Bay Tourism is a membership-based organisation that aims to promote and co-ordinate opportunities for economic growth and prosperity for the visitor industry in Hawke's Bay. And what a job it is, with naturally abundant sunshine and warmth, fresh produce, award-winning wineries and restaurants, luxurious accommodation providers, open spaces set among stunning landscapes, and a wealth of activities and experiences. *hawkesbaynz.com*

GLOSSARY

agar agar a setting agent derived from seaweed. Available from health-food shops.

ascorbic powder also known as L-ascorbic acid. A high concentration of vitamin C in a fine white crystalline powder.

cream, pouring also called pure or fresh cream. It has no additives and contains a minimum fat content of 35 per cent.

crème fraîche a French variation of sour cream, it has a velvety texture and slightly tangy, nutty flavour. It can be boiled without curdling and is used in sweet and savoury dishes.

daikon also called white radish. A long, white radish with a sweet flavour. Eat it raw in salads or shredded as a garnish; also great when sliced or cubed and cooked in stir-fries and casseroles. The flesh is white but the skin can be either white or black.

dashi stock powder dashi is one of the most important ingredients in Japanese cooking, imparting a rich umami flavour to dishes. It is made by steeping kombu, a type of dried kelp, and katsuobushi, a dried and aged tuna, to create a deeply flavoured broth. It is available as instant dashi powder or granules, similar to chicken or beef stock cubes. Dissolve 1-2 teaspoons of dashi powder with 1-2 cups of hot water.

fish sauce also called nam pla or nuoc nam. Made from pulverised salted fermented fish, most often anchovies. Has a very pungent smell and strong taste, so use sparingly.

flour
"00" high-gluten content flour suitable for pasta- and bread-making, which require the gluten component of the flour to be worked in order to provide the necessary structure.
plain unbleached wheat flour is the best for baking: the gluten content ensures a strong dough, which produces a light result.
rice very fine, almost powdery, gluten-free flour. Made from ground white rice. Used in baking, as a thickener, and in some Asian noodles and desserts. Another variety, made from glutinous sweet rice, is used for Chinese dumplings and rice paper.
self-raising all-purpose plain or wholemeal flour with baking powder and salt added. Also called self-rising flour.

tapioca derived from the starchy vegetable cassava root. Often used as an alternative to traditional wheat flours and starches.

gelatine leaves leaf gelatine is tasteless and sets clearer than powdered gelatine, which is why it is preferred by chefs. It is graded according to setting strength, which is measured in 'bloom'. The higher the bloom strength the firmer the set. Each type has a different weight and set so it is advisable to use the type specified in the recipe.
gold-strength we use sheets that are 2.2gm each with a bloom strength of 200.
titanium-strength we use sheets that are 5gm each with a bloom strength of 120.

glucose syrup also known as liquid glucose. Made from wheat starch and used in jam and confectionery making.

glutinous rice a type of rice grown mainly in Southeast and East Asia and the eastern parts of South Asia. The grains are opaque with a very low amylose content and are sticky, or glue-like, when cooked. Used in many forms of Asian cooking, from savoury dishes to desserts.

golden shallots also called French shallots or eschalots. Small and elongated with a brown skin.

Grana Padano Italy's most produced cheese. A full-bodied hard cheese with a grainy, crystalline texture. Aged for a minimum of 9 months, Grana Padano matures more quickly than Parmigiano-Reggiano. It matures in three stages: 9-16 months when it is more delicate in flavour, softer in texture and has a pale yellow colour; 16-20 months when it is grainier with notes of butter, hay and dried fruit; and over 20 months when it has a rich buttery flavour and crystals are present.

grapeseed oil an oil with a high-burn point favoured by chefs due its neutral taste.

isomalt powder a substitute sugar made from beet sugar. White in colour, crystalline and odourless, it needs to be melted down in order to be used. Technically derived from sugar, it has a much lower calorie and carbohydrate count, and has only about 65 per cent of the sweetness of sugar. Isomalt is an extremely stable sugar substitute.

juniper berries dried berries of an evergreen tree, it is the main flavouring ingredient in gin.

katsuobushi dried bonito flakes.

kawakawa leaves dark green, heart-shaped leaves from the kawakawa plant, native to New Zealand. Traditionally, the leaves were used to brew herbal remedies or concoctions. The leaves have a peppery bitter taste and can have a numbing effect on the mouth if eaten in large enough quantities.

kohlrabi related to cabbage with a cabbage-like smell and the taste of broccoli stems. Bulbous with long leafy greens that shoot out from the top, kohlrabi can be green or purple. All parts can be eaten, both raw and cooked. It can be steamed, sautéed, roasted, stuffed, creamed and cubed in soups or stews.

kombu a form of edible kelp widely used in Japanese cooking to make broths. It can also be pickled, eaten fresh and deep-fried.

kūmara (orange sweet potato) the Polynesian name of an orange-fleshed sweet potato often confused with yam. Good baked, boiled, mashed or fried similarly to other potatoes.

lemongrass a tall, clumping, lemon-smelling and -tasting, sharp-edged aromatic tropical grass. The white lower part of the stem is used in many Southeast Asian dishes.

lemon verbena leaves a slightly sweet, bright, herbaceous, lemon-scented herb with a number of uses, ranging from savoury to sweet. Commonly used to flavour fruit-based drinks, dressings, fish soups, marinades, puddings, jams and desserts. Pairs well with fruits, vanilla and seafood dishes.

makrut lime leaf sold fresh, dried or frozen, it looks like two glossy dark green leaves joined end to end, forming a rounded hourglass shape. A strip of fresh lime peel may be substituted for each makrut lime leaf.

mānuka honey made in Australia and New Zealand by bees that pollinate the flower leptospermum scoparium bush (also known as the mānuka bush). It has antibacterial, antiviral and anti-inflammatory properties, and a unique, strong, slightly earthy and bitter taste.

mānuka wood chips an all-round robust-flavoured wood chip that complements all meats but is particularly good with seafood. With a higher density than most other smoking hardwoods, it produces a heavy smoke with a hint of sweetness.

matcha tea powder green tea leaves stoneground into a fine powdered form. Matcha has up to 137 times the antioxidants and up to 10 times the nutritional content of regular green tea.

mirin a Japanese champagne-coloured cooking wine made of glutinous rice and alcohol.

mizuna a mild-flavoured Japanese mustard green that is commonly grown for commercial salad mixes. It has feathery, serrated leaves and a mildly peppery taste.

nasturtium leaves an edible flower available in a range of hues. Both the leaf and flower have a peppery bite similar to a radish.

'nduja a soft, spreadable fermented pork salume, spiked with fiery Calabrian chillies.

nori sheets a type of dried seaweed used in Japanese cooking as a flavouring, garnish or for sushi. Sold in thin sheets, plain or toasted (yaki-nori).

panko breadcrumbs also called Japanese breadcrumbs. Available in two kinds: larger pieces and fine crumbs. They have a lighter texture than Western-style breadcrumbs.

Pernod a French anise-flavoured pastis apéritif.

pickled ginger pink or red coloured pickled paper-thin shavings of ginger in a mixture of vinegar, sugar and natural colouring. Used in Japanese cooking.

pomegranate molasses not to be confused with pomegranate syrup or grenadine (used in cocktails). Pomegranate molasses is thicker, browner, and more concentrated in flavour – tart and sharp, slightly sweet and fruity.

saffron stigma of a member of the crocus family, available ground or in strands. Imparts a yellow-orange colour to food once infused. The quality can vary greatly; the best is the most expensive spice in the world.

sake made from fermented rice. Used for marinating, cooking and as part of dipping sauces. Substitute dry sherry, vermouth or brandy.

Sichuan peppercorns also called Szechuan or Chinese pepper, native to the Sichuan province of China. A mildly hot spice that comes from the prickly ash tree. Although not related to the peppercorn family, small, red-brown aromatic Sichuan berries look like black peppercorns and have a distinctive peppery-lemon flavour and aroma.

shiso the Japanese name for a popular Southeast Asian herb. A member of the mint family, it has jagged leaves and a flavour similar to basil and coriander with subtle hints of cumin and cloves. Served fresh or pickled and commonly used to garnish sushi and other Japanese dishes.

sugar
coconut made from the nectar of coconut blossoms from coconut palms, with a caramel taste and crumb-like texture.
golden caster sugar a fine granulated sugar made from unrefined sugar cane or beets. Light golden in colour and similar in texture to regular white caster sugar, it has a subtle buttery, caramel flavour. If a recipe calls for regular white caster sugar, you can substitute for golden caster sugar.
muscovado an unrefined cane sugar that contains natural molasses. It has a rich brown colour, moist texture and strong molasses flavour.
palm also called nam tan pip, jaggery, jawa or gula melaka. Made from the sap of the sugar palm tree. Light brown to black in colour and usually sold in rock-hard cakes.

Substitute brown sugar if unavailable.
rapadura an unbleached and unrefined whole cane sugar that is higher in minerals and antioxidants than regular white sugar. It has a high molasses content, which gives it its characteristic caramel-like colour.

sumac a purple-red, astringent spice ground from berries growing on shrubs that flourish wild around the Mediterranean. Adds a tart, lemony flavour to dips and dressings and goes well with barbecued meat.

tamarind purée (or paste) the commercial result of the distillation of tamarind juice into a condensed, compacted purée.

verjuice the unfermented juice from unripe grapes.

vinegar
chardonnay made from Chardonnay wine. Fruity with a delicate, complex flavour.
raspberry made from raspberry juice, vinegar and sugar, it has a refreshing, tangy and fruity flavour.
sherry a Spanish vinegar made from fermenting sherry wine. It has a deep, complex flavour and subtle caramel notes, with less acidity than red or white wine vinegar.

sturgeon caviar the matured eggs of the fish sturgeon, which is the common name for the 27 species of fish belonging to the family Acipenseridae. There are various species of sturgeon fish living in the fresh waters of the northern hemisphere. Roe, the general word for fish eggs, which could come from any type of fish, is not caviar.

white truffle a particular species of truffle called tuber magnatum, it is available a couple of months of the year, almost exclusively from one part of Italy, most famously in the countryside around the cities of Alba. More fragrant and flavourful than black truffles, Italian white truffles are highly desired and the most valuable.

xanthan gum derived from fermenting sugar with a form of bacteria. Used as a multi-use stabiliser and thickener. It has no discernible taste and a pleasing mouthfeel.

COOK'S NOTES

Measures & equipment

- All cup and spoon measures are level and based on Australian metric measures.
- Eggs have an average weight of 59gm unless otherwise specified.
- Fruit and vegetables are washed, peeled and medium-sized unless specified.
- Oven temperatures are for conventional ovens and need to be adjusted for fan-forced ovens.
- Pans are medium-sized and heavy-based; cake tins are stainless steel, unless otherwise specified.

Cooking tips

- When seasoning food, we use sea salt and freshly ground pepper.
- To blanch an ingredient, cook it briefly in boiling water, then drain. To refresh, plunge in iced water, then drain.
- We recommend using free-range eggs, chicken and pork. We use female pork for preference.
- Makrut lime leaves are also known as kaffir lime leaves.
- Unless specified, neutral oil means any of grapeseed, canola, sunflower or vegetable oil.
- To dry-roast spices, cook them in a dry pan, stirring over medium-high heat until fragrant. Cooking time varies.
- Non-reactive bowls are made from glass, ceramic or plastic. Use them in preference to metal bowls when marinating to prevent the acid in marinades reacting with metal and imparting a metallic taste.
- SPCA New Zealand recommends people source crustaceans, including crayfish, crabs and lobster from a place where they have been humanely killed by trained and competent personnel, using the methods outlined in our position statement, before purchase. www.spca.nz/advice-and-welfare/article/aquatic-crustaceans-caught-and-used-for-food
- All herbs are fresh, with leaves and tender stems used, unless specified.
- Eggwash is lightly beaten egg used for glazing or sealing.
- Sugar syrup is made of equal parts sugar and water, unless otherwise specified. Bring mixture to the boil to dissolve sugar, remove from heat and cool before use.
- Acidulated water is a mixture of water and lemon juice.
- To sterilise jars and lids, run them through the hot rinse cycle in a dishwasher, or wash them in hot soapy water, rinse well, place on a tray in a cold oven and heat at 120°C for 30 minutes.
- To blind bake, line a pastry-lined tart tin with baking paper, then fill it with weights (ceramic weights, rice and dried beans work best).
- To clarify butter, cook it over low heat until the fat and the milk solids separate. Strain off the clear butter and discard the milk solids. You will lose about 20 per cent of the volume in milk solids.

INDEX

Published in 2022 by Are Media Books, Australia. Are Media Books is a division of Are Media Pty Ltd.

Editor Joanna Hunkin

Food Director Sophia Young

Creative Director Hannah Blackmore

Managing Editor Stephanie Kistner

Content Editors Suzanna Chriss, Michelle Oalin (recipes)

Senior Food Editor Dominic Smith

Project Coordinator Georgia Moore

Head of Operations David Scotto

Business Development Director Joe Revill

Business Development Manager Amanda Atkinson

A catalogue record for this book is available from the National Library of Australia. ISBN 978-1-76122-047-0

FOOD PHOTOGRAPHY

Photographer William Meppem

Stylist Lucy Tweed

Photochef Jimmy Callaway

Photochef Assistants Clare Maguire, Vikki Moursellas

Recipe Testing Max Adey, Olivia Andrews, Rebecca Lyall, Kerrie Worner

Wine Matches Samantha Payne

TRAVEL PHOTOGRAPHY

Daniel Murray Photography (p2-3)

The publisher would like to thank Devitt Meats for supplying all the meat in this book.

DEVITT
WHOLESALE MEATS

Published by Are Media Books, a division of Are Media Pty Limited, 54 Park St, Sydney; GPO Box 4088, Sydney, NSW 2001, Australia
Phone +61 2 9282 8000
aremediabooks.com.au

Published in partnership with
Southern Crossings
southern-crossings.com

To order books
Phone 1300 322 007 (within Australia)
Or online at aremediabooks.com.au

Printed in China by
C&C Offset Printing Co., Ltd

FSC
www.fsc.org
MIX
Paper from responsible sources
FSC® C008047

SOUTHERN CROSSINGS